Step-by-Step Chakra Healing for Beginners

Open, Heal, and Harness the Power of Your Chakras

Travis Hemingway

© **Copyright 2022 Travis Hemingway - All rights reserved.**

The content contained within this book may not be reproduced, duplicated or transmitted without direct written permission from the author or the publisher.

Under no circumstances will any blame or legal responsibility be held against the publisher, or author, for any damages, reparation, or monetary loss due to the information contained within this book, either directly or indirectly.

Legal Notice:
This book is copyright protected. It is only for personal use. You cannot amend, distribute, sell, use, quote or paraphrase any part, or the content within this book, without the consent of the author or publisher.

Disclaimer Notice:
Please note the information contained within this document is for educational and entertainment purposes only. All effort has been executed to present accurate, up to date, reliable, complete information. No warranties of any kind are declared or implied. Readers acknowledge that the author is not engaged in the rendering of legal, financial, medical or professional advice. The content within this book has been derived from various sources. Please consult a licensed professional before attempting any techniques outlined in this book.

By reading this document, the reader agrees that under no circumstances is the author responsible for any losses, direct or indirect, that are incurred as a result of the use of the information contained within this document, including, but not limited to, errors, omissions, or inaccuracies.

Table of Contents

Introduction	1
Chapter 1 Chakra Healing—Working With Energy	5
Understanding Energy Healing	6
Busting the Myths Around Energy Healing	7
Different Kinds of Energy Healing	12
Chapter 2 Chakra Healing—Concepts, Myths, and Benefits	17
The Subtle Body	17
The Energy Pathways for the Vital Life Force	19
The Concept of Chakras	20
Busting the Myths Around Chakras	21
A Deeper Understanding of the Seven Chakras	29
Chapter 3 An Introduction to Kundalini Energy	36
What Is Kundalini?	36
How Does A Kundalini Awakening Occur?	38
Benefits of Kundalini Awakening	39
Issues Related to Kundalini Awakening	41
Symptoms of Kundalini Awakening	44
Should You Try to Initiate a Kundalini Awakening?	48
Chapter 4 The Effects of Imbalanced Chakras on Your Life	51
How Do You Know If Your Chakras Are Imbalanced?	51
Imbalance in the Root Chakra	57
Imbalance in the Sacral Chakra	58

Imbalance in the Solar Plexus Chakra	59
Imbalance in the Heart Chakra	60
Imbalance in the Throat Chakra	61
Imbalance in the Third Eye Chakra	62
Imbalance in the Crown Chakra	63
Chapter 5 Giving Your Inner Self The Things It Needs Most	65
Getting to Know Yourself	66
Benefits of Chakra Healing	70
Chapter 6 Learning How to Balance Your Chakras	75
The Two Dimensions of Our Chakras	76
The Path to Chakra Healing	77
Methods for Balancing Your Chakras	79
Chakra Meditation and Visualization	79
The Importance of Sound in Chakra Healing	81
Crystal Healing	84
Essential Oils for Chakra Healing	87
Chapter 7 How to Heal Your Root Chakra	89
Meditation Practice	89
Grounding Practices	90
Affirmations	91
Yoga Practices	92
Crystal Healing	92
Essential Oils	93
Chapter 8 How to Heal Your Sacral Chakra	94
Meditation Practice	94

Healing Through Water	95
Affirmations	95
Yoga Practices	96
Crystal Healing	96
Essential Oils	97
Chapter 9 How to Heal Your Solar Plexus Chakra	99
Meditation Practice	99
Channeling the Power of the Sun	100
Affirmations	101
Yoga Practices	101
Crystal Healing	101
Essential Oils	102
Chapter 10 How to Heal Your Heart Chakra	103
Meditation Practice	103
Learning to Love Again	104
Affirmations	104
Yoga Practices	105
Crystal Healing	106
Essential Oils	106
Chapter 11 How to Heal Your Throat Chakra	108
Meditation Practice	108
Meeting Your Authentic Self	109
Affirmations	110
Yoga Practices	110
Crystal Healing	110

Essential Oils	111
Chapter 12 Common Mistakes Made on The Healing Journey	112
Don't Rush, Don't Compare	112
Be Aware of the Energies in Your Environment	113
Be Aware of, And Protect Your Energy	113
Not Being True to Yourself	114
Conclusion	115
References	118

Words From the Author

Hey, it's Travis. Thank you so much for giving me a chance to make an impact in your life. I feel its my *mission* to help guide anyone and everyone who is looking for an answer. I find it important that I share what I've learned on my journey thus far. Hopefully, by doing so, you all won't have to feel as lost as I once did. That's all for now and I hope I'm able to help.

Feel free to check out my other books here:

https://www.amazon.com/author/travishemingway

Claim your **FREE** gift by scanning the code below.

Introduction

Without knowing energy, you cannot approach your soul. –Ilchi Lee

Vivian is exhausted. She works in a high-paced and competitive environment. That, coupled with the fact that she is bringing up three kids under the age of seven with her partner, means that she's used to feeling tired and overwhelmed now and then. This, however, is something insidious. Not only does she feel perpetually depleted, but also feels disconnected from everyone around her.

Earlier, when something made her feel stressed or tired, she reminded herself why she was doing it in the first place. Usually, spending time with her children and partner, or being recognized by her colleagues and superiors was enough to make her feel motivated again. This time, nothing is helping her. She loves her children more than anything in the world but can't get herself to connect with them the way she used to. She's also less confident about her ability to see her current professional projects to completion.

What makes the situation worse for her is that she cannot pinpoint where these feelings and behaviors are emanating from. This makes her feel even more helpless about finding a solution to her problems. It has also become difficult to communicate her concerns with the people closest to her. What can she say, except "it feels like something is off?" That doesn't give anyone a lot to go on, does it?

Vivian's case is not an isolated one. All of us go through these phases in which nothing seems to make sense, and when we feel as if our body and mind are betraying us. Of late, humanity as a whole has been grappling with far more than it is used to. Be it physically, mentally, economically, politically, or spiritually—the challenges don't seem to end. If you talk to people around you, or if you follow discussions on social media and virtual platforms, chances are, most people will admit to feeling extraordinarily lost and depleted. This is the case even if they seem to be physically fine. Of course, some people have faced greater challenges than others, but almost no one has been left unscathed by the wave of helplessness, anxiety, and fatigue that has swept the globe.

It might seem like there's no end in sight. It surely felt that way to me, until I shifted my perspective and started understanding myself in terms of energy. For me, *chakra* healing has been a way to improve my physical, mental, and spiritual health. It has also made it possible for me to uncover my true purpose, come into balance with myself, and unlock my inner power. Of course, none of this has been easy, nor is my transformation complete by any means. That being said, understanding how chakras work has given me the confidence that I'm following the path that I'm meant to. As someone who knows how it feels to be lost, I want to help others to get in touch with their true selves through chakra healing.

I am Travis Hemingway, and I've written this book for people who want to change their lives from within, but don't know where to start. Maybe you've never heard of the concept of chakra healing. Maybe you have an idea of the same, but find it intimidating. Maybe you're unsure of your ability to work with your energy. I have written this book to cater to anyone who has just started their journey.

In this book, we will understand what chakras are and how they play a role in every aspect of our lives. We'll try to understand each chakra, as well as its functions, at a deeper level. Why should you keep your chakras balanced? What happens when your chakras are thrown out of balance? What is *kundalini* awakening? How does energy flow through our bodies? How can we learn to control and channel our energies in such a way that it helps us create our destinies? These are some of the questions that this book seeks to answer.

We'll understand the origins of this concept, and why it's useful to us even if we're not spiritually inclined. We'll see how chakras affect every aspect of our lives—physical, mental, emotional, sexual, and spiritual. We'll also discuss how we can balance our chakras through diet, meditation, crystals, essential oils, and behavioral changes within ourselves.

Our inner world is as vast as it is mysterious. It takes a lot of time and patience to understand this world. Without proper guidance, we might lose ourselves in this world. The purpose of this book isn't to become your guide as much as it is to help awaken your inner compass so that you can navigate the world as your true self. There are many paths to spiritual awakening, and you should only follow the path that resonates with you. Therefore, this book will also help you ask the questions that are important for you to discover your path. Most importantly, it will help you stay away from false or misleading information that can be presented to people who are beginning their journey.

This is because, as rewarding as this journey is, it can also be challenging. If you're not sure of who you are, and what your purpose is in this world, you might give up easily. As beginners, you need encouragement as well as the knowledge that you can rely on at all times. This book aims to provide you with both. I hope that armed with the information presented here, you will be able to begin this exhilarating journey with confidence.

Chapter 1
Chakra Healing—Working With Energy

Many spiritual leaders believe that we are spiritual beings living in a material world. Some cultures and schools of thought place great importance on the spiritual quest and the spiritual life. Others believe that a material life lived with meaning is all that is needed for our lives to be considered successful. For many of us, especially in the Western world, it can be difficult to think in terms of energy. After all, we're taught to question everything that is taught to us and to always look for concrete proof in whatever's presented to us. Sometimes, this also means that we consider spirituality as being antithetical to science.

However, in many ancient traditions, science and spirituality aren't incompatible. They're seen as different pathways to the same truth. Some *gurus* even believe that what you come across on your spiritual journey will be understood by science in due time. Now, what does this mean to you? What if you're not particularly spiritual but still want to understand energy healing? What if you don't know anything about energy healing but want to try anything that might help you improve your physical and mental health? The good news is, energy healing is a great first step to take even if you're a complete novice.

In the chapter, we'll try to understand the energy body that is present within each one of us, and how we can use this knowledge to heal ourselves holistically. All you need is an open and curious mind.

Understanding Energy Healing

Whether you've come across the term or not, chances are, you've already experienced the effects of energy in your own life. For example, if you've just met someone but don't "vibe" with them, you're responding to their energy. Similarly, if you go to a place you've never been to before, and feel like "something's off," you've picked something about that place based on the energy it gives off. Of course, some people are more adept at this than others. For example, empaths and/or highly sensitive people (HSPs) can perceive things that aren't obvious. They tend to absorb the energies of the people around them, their environment, and even the zeitgeist.

On one hand, this makes them vulnerable to feeling overwhelmed and tired, and might even create challenges in dealing with the world. On the other hand, if they can learn to channel their instincts and tap into energies in a constructive manner, they can help themselves as well as many others.

In many ancient traditions, our bodies and minds are seen as possessing different frequencies and energies that can be worked with for our benefit. Of late, modern medicine has begun to realize the importance of energy healing in providing holistic treatment to patients and ensuring that people achieve mind-body balance in their daily lives.

For this, we need to pinpoint the things that are making our lives difficult. Think about it this way. If energy is present within our body, mind, and soul, then it needs to be flowing smoothly. Similarly, if we're vibrating at a certain frequency, we want that frequency to be high.

Nevertheless, when we interact with the world, our energies are also influenced. Sometimes, we might be vibrating at a lower frequency level than is good for us. Other times, our energy might be blocked. In both these cases, we might be experiencing physical, mental, and emotional problems.

One of the reasons why healing ourselves from these "energy blocks" is so difficult is that we don't even know what we're looking for. This is especially true if we seem to be physically fine but aren't internally healthy. When we start our energy healing process, the first thing to do is to get intimate with our subconscious mind. This isn't easy, but this is where we begin to get the answers we're looking for. When we begin to uncover our thoughts and patterns, we'll also understand anything that might be holding us back.

This is also important because physical, mental, and emotional health are often intertwined with each other. For example, if you don't healthily deal with stress, or if you have anger issues, it can affect your blood pressure and heart health. Now, these anger issues might stem from your experiences in the past or certain repressed traumas. These can cause blocks within your body and mind, leading to numerous issues. Through energy healing, we can identify and heal these issues, thus improving our health on all levels.

Busting the Myths Around Energy Healing

As powerful and transformative energy healing can be, there are roadblocks to its widespread success. The biggest problem with this practice is the lack of faith that most people have. Since this is a relatively new concept for most people in the Western world, it can take some time for them to be comfortable with it. The other issue is that, in the absence of reliable sources of information, many people might become susceptible to so-called "healers" who aren't fully equipped to work with energy. Some of these people might intentionally cause harm, but most others might do so with the noblest intentions. This is why it's important to bust certain myths around energy healing.

Myth 1: Energy healing is unscientific.

Fact: This is the most common complaint that people have with energy healing. Certain things need to be emphasized to dispel this myth. First, there are prestigious health institutions in the US that have been conducting scientific inquiry and research in this field. These include institutions such as the National Center for Health Statistics (NCHS), National Center for Complementary and Integrative Health (NCCIH), and National Center for Complementary and Alternative Medicine (NCCAM).

Many such institutions have been trying to understand the efficacy and safety of energy healing. It's becoming clearer than ever that energy healing can help us deal with mental and emotional health issues, and can also help us in treating physical ailments. While the scope of energy healing is immense, and many practitioners believe that its foremost aim is in elevating our consciousness, people who are looking to benefit in material ways will not be disappointed.

It does take a perspective shift to welcome energy healing into our lives, but this shift is a rewarding one. If you need any more assurance, Nikola Tesla, one of the greatest scientific minds of all time, once said, "If you want to find the secrets of the universe, think in terms of energy, frequency, and vibration (Tesla, n.d.)."

Myth 2: Energy healing is for the religious-minded.

Fact: You don't have to subscribe to a particular religion or school of thought to benefit from energy healing. It certainly helps if you believe in spirituality, or if you want to dedicate your journey to a Higher Power. This can give you strength, and it can also help you understand some of the paths that spiritual leaders take when working with energy. For example, some ancient beliefs such as Hinduism talk about the possibility of union with the Higher Consciousness. They see all energy work as an attempt toward this union.

You might have different views on this, or you might not want religion to feature on your journey. That's okay. If you want, you can think of energy as something that powers all your life processes. You can look at energy as something that you can control for your health. You can see this process as something that offers you a chance to understand yourself deeply. If the only universe you're interested in is within you, energy healing is a worthwhile endeavor for you.

Myth 3: Energy healing cannot be done without a practitioner.

Fact: Even though the original practices might have followed a particular set of beliefs, you can always tweak them in a manner you see fit. Of course, some paths require that you have a spiritual teacher by your side when you undertake the journey, but you can choose a path that agrees with your intuition. There are many forms of energy healing, and it's advisable to understand exactly what each form entails. That being said, you can certainly take this journey on your own, provided you have the right information on hand.

It's important to remember that there are so-called teachers who use these practices to dupe unsuspecting people. Also, since energy healing can involve a lot of vulnerability, it's really important to choose practitioners whom you can trust on this journey. The most important thing to remember (and I will be reminding you of this throughout the book) is that all forms of healing derive power from your internal landscape and the will you possess. Even the best teachers can only guide you; you're the one who needs to take this journey.

Myth 4: Energy healing is either irrelevant and outdated, or its New Age hogwash.

Fact: I've addressed the two together because they're two sides to the same argument—that energy healing is ineffective and an illusion. If it's seen as something old, it's easier for people to believe that it belongs to a time when people weren't knowledgeable or educated enough to know better than to believe in such practices. Similarly, if it's a part of New Age practices, it belongs to the "hippie culture" that is often accused of appropriating ancient beliefs for its own self-purpose. Either way, the message is clear: Don't waste your time with it.

The fact is, neither of these statements is entirely accurate. Yes, many energy healing practices originate in ancient cultures in India, China, Japan, and so on. However, discarding these practices as those borne out of ignorance is as juvenile as it's arrogant. When we look at various historical records, we see that our forefathers had astounding amounts of knowledge in art, architecture, music, and literature. Even with fewer resources than those available to us today, they made remarkable strides in every field. This is why it's premature to dismiss their practices and knowledge simply because we can't understand them fully.

When it comes to the modern takes on energy healing, let me just say that there's nothing wrong with evolving practices, as long as people are respectful and aware of their origins. As long as these practices benefit people, we should keep an open mind about them. Of course, we should use our sense of discernment wherever possible, and only commit to those practices that resonate with us. As unreasonable as it is to blindly follow a practice, it's equally immature to reject something without fully understanding it. By this, I don't mean that you can ever completely understand the energetic realm. What I mean is that you find enough information (both explicit and implicit) to have faith in yourself while you begin this journey.

Myth 5: Energy healing can mess with your energy or drain your energy.

Fact: To understand this, try to draw a parallel with traditional healing methods. If you don't administer the proper medicines or treatments, you might suffer from side effects or other issues. Also, even the correct course of treatment might make you feel a little under the weather while it does its work. The same goes for alternative methods. Since you're working with energy, you should understand how different practices can affect your energy levels and quality. It might take some time for you to understand what works for you and what doesn't. This doesn't make it problematic or objectively bad for you.

Also, when we begin to work with energy, most of the healing requires that we face our innermost fears, traumas, and blocks. This isn't an easy process. In many cases, it involves a dissolution of our ego (more on this later). Therefore, it's understandable that, as we begin to free the energy within ourselves of the constraints we've unknowingly placed on it, our bodies will react in different ways. Sometimes, after a particularly intense session, we might feel temporarily fatigued. Other times, we might experience an inexplicable surge of energy. After a while, these changes will resolve on their own. Also, it's important to note that if you feel any kind of discomfort, you should always talk to your doctor. You shouldn't see energy healing as a substitute for traditional medicine.

That being said, energy healing doesn't require you to "surrender" your energy to a practitioner or the universe at any stage. If anything, it helps you take charge of your energy and your life.

Different Kinds of Energy Healing

As energy healing is accepted by more medical practitioners around the world, we have more options available to us than ever before. As such, it can be overwhelming for someone who is just starting on this journey. Let's discuss different kinds of energy healing techniques for us to choose from.

- **Light and sound healing:** Both light and sound carry frequencies that can be used for healing. Different sounds and lights (including colors) include different vibrations that can help remove the different blocks in our bodies. They can also help soothe us emotionally and spiritually, thus making it easier for us to tap into our hidden potential. A popular form of sound healing these days uses Tibetan singing bowls. Both sound and light can also be used to cleanse the physical spaces we occupy, thus making it easier for us to balance our bodies and minds.

- **Grounding:** Also known as earthing, this technique is used to help us reconnect to the earth. It's believed that when our bodies touch the earth in an intentional and meaningful manner, the healing energy of the earth transfers to us and helps us heal ourselves. Since this is a relatively new practice, the scientific evidence supporting it is few and far between. Even so, this is a promising new area of research for holistic practitioners. Even intuitively, you might experience the benefits of grounding yourself. Some of the simplest ways of doing so are by touching the earth—for example, by walking barefoot on grass, or by lying down on the ground (in a safe space). You can also benefit from this practice by soaking your feet in the water or even swimming in a natural body of water (with the appropriate precautions). Each of these methods opens us to the healing properties of the earth and water.

- **Movement:** In almost every ancient culture, meaningful movement has been crucial to the preservation and channeling of the vital life force present in our bodies. Known as *prana*, chi, or qi, this life force is important for our emotional, mental, and physical well-being. Therefore, different techniques can help this energy flow unimpeded in our mind-body systems. Some of these forms include yoga, *pranayama*, *qi gong*, and *tai chi*. Most of these practices combine breathwork, meditation, visualization, and different forms of movement that help release internal blocks, improve overall health and well-being, and bring us closer to our true selves. Even if you don't follow any of these practices, you can still include mindful movement in your routine in the form of walking, running, or even dancing.

- **Reiki:** Reiki is an ancient Japanese healing technique that also works on the principle of channeling the universal life force in such a way that it helps heal us. This is a practice in which a healer lets the healing energy flow through their hands into the person being healed (either through touch or near touch). Once this healing energy reaches us, all the blocked life force (which is the cause for numerous emotional, physical, and mental processes) starts flowing freely again.

- **Acupuncture:** An ancient Chinese healing technique, acupuncture helps to ease physical discomfort and pain (among other things) through the strategic use of needles on a person's body. This is one of the practices that have become mainstream in the medical community with a credible body of research behind it. This holds promise for other, lesser-known but equally effective, techniques in the future. The practice of acupuncture is linked to the concept of energy meridians, along which our vital energy (life force) flows. When a patient complains of pain or stiffness in a certain part of their body, the practitioner determines the corresponding energy meridian for that part and then places needles along that meridian to help the blocked energy flow smoothly.

- **Aromatherapy:** This practice uses essential oils extracted from various herbs and plants to use for healing purposes. These oils, which can either be applied to different points of our bodies or diffused into the atmosphere, help in improving our moods, relaxing us, and also relieving physical, mental, and emotional stress in our lives. Some of these oils can also help with improving our sleep cycles. Many people opt for massages using aromatherapy oils. The concept behind this practice states that each plant has its vibrational energy, and this energy affects humans when they ingest, inhale, or even touch them.

- **Chakra healing:** This is a practice that has originated in ancient Vedic traditions, in which the life force (known as prana) is said to accumulate at different points in the energy body. These points are known as chakras, and they carry codes for leading a richer and more balanced life—physically, mentally, and emotionally. Originally, chakra healing was a way to connect to the Divine Source, but modern takes on this practice have expanded the practice to help people improve their lives materially as well.

Now that we know about the most prominent energy healing practices available to us, there are a few things that we should keep in mind before we begin our journey. First, most of these methods don't show you overnight results, and even if they do, they need time for any changes to be permanent. So you need patience and faith throughout the process.

Second, if you're choosing a practice that needs a guide or practitioner to help you along the way, you must do your due diligence and conduct proper research before committing to that practitioner. As I've mentioned before, some of these people might be frauds. Others might be well-intentioned but lack the necessary training and qualifications. And still, others might be extremely well-qualified but not suitable for you. Think of it as choosing a therapist for yourself. It takes time (and sometimes, trial and error) to land on the perfect person for your therapeutic journey. Energy healing shouldn't be any different.

Third, you might be tempted to try out as many practices as can in the beginning. This isn't advisable. Each practice has its own set of beliefs and concepts. Even if many of these concepts overlap with and complement each other, it's a good idea to start with one or two of them, and then add others to your practice if needed, Since you're working with energy, you might also find yourself becoming overwhelmed and fatigued if you deal with many practices at the same time.

Fourth, energy healing practices show the best results when combined with diet, exercise, and other holistic healing methods. Keep your primary healthcare physician in the loop when you start any new practice and always try to establish a balance in your daily routine.

Now that we have a basic idea of energy healing, let's focus on understanding what chakras are, and why they're important for our mental, physical, and emotional health.

Chapter 2

Chakra Healing—Concepts, Myths, and Benefits

In the last chapter, we talked about the different forms of energy healing that we can explore. Many of these practices are informed by each other, simply because most of them work on the understanding of a vital life force and a subtle body. Intriguingly, different cultures and schools of thought have arrived at similar conclusions regarding the subtle body.

In this chapter, we'll discuss the subtle body in some detail, as its understanding forms the basis of our chakra healing journey. Much like yoga, meditation, and mindfulness, chakra healing has become a much-discussed topic among practitioners and spiritual seekers in the West. Sometimes, it might feel like there's too much information out there, which can be overwhelming for a beginner. At the same time, we must have the correct information and the right context before we decide if this practice is for us. This chapter will help us understand the basic concepts behind chakras, the origins of this concept, the myths surrounding it, and the benefits that this journey can bestow on you.

The Subtle Body

The subtle, or energy body has an important place in many Eastern traditions. Simply put, this body acts as a bridge between the material and spiritual planes of existence, belonging to neither plane entirely. Since chakras originate in Vedic traditions (of Hinduism), we'll try to understand the subtle body in the same traditions.

In Hinduism, a human being is said to possess different layers (or *koshas*) of being. Each layer performs a different function—physical, mental, emotional, intellectual, spiritual, and so on. We also have three bodies—the gross or physical body (*karya sharira*), the causal body (*karana sharira*), and the subtle body (*sukshma sharira*). The physical body is what we know and usually works with all our lives.

This is the body that carries both the subtle and the causal bodies. It is said to be made up of the five elements—air, fire, water, earth, and ether—and experiences life, aging, death, and decay in this world. Since Hinduism supports the idea of reincarnation, it's believed that the physical body is the one that no longer exists when we die. In other words, it's treated as a perishable vessel for your essential bodies.

The causal body is supposed to be the one that carries our soul, or Consciousness. This is a complex body of which a lot is yet to be understood. This body is believed to survive death, and reincarnates, often in a new body. It's also through this body that our consciousness can merge with the Universal Consciousness.

We now come to the subtle body, which is the body that's supposed to house our vital life force, as well as our mind and intellect. In Hinduism, this vital life force is known as prana. To keep this prana balanced, meditation, yoga, and pranayama need to be practiced regularly. In simple terms, pranayama is the practice of controlling this vital life force. When we learn to do this well, we can automatically improve our vital energy levels.

We'll discuss this in detail when we talk about balancing our chakras.

Now that we know how important the subtle body and our vital life force are, let's talk about the energy pathways that circulate this life force throughout our subtle bodies.

The Energy Pathways for the Vital Life Force

If there's energy, it needs to flow unrestricted throughout our bodies, right? Before we go deeper into this topic, I would like to make it clear that our subtle body doesn't exist on the physical plane. This means that, if we're looking for exact physical manifestations of this body or the pathways that carry our vital energies, we won't find them. This can take some getting used to, but the important thing to remember is that this subtle body has a very tangible effect on our physical realities.

Now, remember our discussion about energy meridians when we talked about acupuncture? These meridians are nothing but channels through which the vital energy flows. In Hinduism, these channels are known as *nadis*. There are 72,000 nadis in our subtle body, and they spring from three basic ones—*ida, pingala,* and *sushumna*. While ida is the left channel, pingala is the right one.

We can also look at these channels in terms of the dual energies that govern life. For example, ida can also represent the Divine Feminine energy (known as *Shakti*), while pingala represents the Divine Masculine energy (known as *Shiva*). Here, it's important to mention that masculine and feminine are not understood in terms of the gender constructs that we're used to on the physical plane. Rather, they're understood as energies. For example, the masculine energy or the pingala can represent a more logical side of us, while the feminine side or ida refers to the intuitive one. All of us have both masculine and feminine energies present within us. The important thing is to maintain a balance between these two energies.

Now, you might be wondering about the sushumna nadi. This is the most important energy pathway in our subtle bodies. In fact, for the most balanced and pure state of mind, we need our life force to be moving freely through this channel. For most people, the sushumna nadi doesn't even come into the picture all their lives. In other words, the energy or potential within it lies dormant.

Now that we know how energy moves within our subtle body, let's understand what chakras are.

The Concept of Chakras

Chakras as a concept were first introduced in the *Vedas*, specifically in the *Yoga Upanishads*. Later, the *tantric* school of thought helped me to understand the concept in great detail. As there are different schools of thought, there are different ways of explaining chakras. First, the word chakra comes from Sanskrit, where it translates to "wheel." Some schools of thought look at chakras as "disks or wheels of energy" that are continuously spinning.

Others believe that chakras are triangular. Keep in mind that none of these can be physically seen in the body. We're only talking about them in representational terms. One thing that everyone agrees on is that these chakras are the meeting point of different nadis. In that sense, these chakras are the points where energy pools in our subtle body.

Now, these chakras are conceptual, but they are said to be based on different points along our spine. This is for two reasons. One, when we discuss this concept with others, we need reference points for them to understand what we're talking about. If everyone has their understanding of where these chakras reside, it wouldn't work.

Second, and more importantly, the points at which these chakras are said to be based are those points where certain emotions emanate within us. Therefore, when we say that a particular chakra is based somewhere along our body, what we mean is that we feel a particular emotion (or have a particular experience) at that point in our body. More accurately, those points influence our experiences in the material world.

Since these concepts can be a little tricky to understand for beginners (and can even confuse more experienced learners), let's discuss them differently. We'll look at some of the common myths that surround chakras and dispel them to get a clearer picture of this concept.

Busting the Myths Around Chakras

Myth 1: Chakras don't exist, or they don't have a basis in reality.

Fact: This is a myth that somehow persists even today, mostly in the Western world. The reason is that our rational minds cannot quite grasp a concept that cannot be verified physically. For example, when we talk about the different organs or glands in our bodies, we know that these exist anatomically. This is not the case with chakras. However, this doesn't mean that they don't exist, just that they exist on a plane that we're not used to comprehending.

When it comes to their effects on the material world, we know by now that these conceptual structures can have very real effects on our bodies, minds, emotions, and relationships. Since most of us are distant from our intuitive selves, it can be difficult to understand that this concept is real, but years of spiritual teachings, as well as the testimonials of people who have been affected by chakra healing, should convince us.

Myth 2: Chakras are physical entities that can be located along the physical spine.

Fact: This is almost the opposite of the first myth, but is equally problematic. This myth might also originate from our desire to give a tangible basis to this concept. To be clear, you won't "find" a chakra as a gland or a disc along the spine. As I mentioned earlier, certain points are seen as the locations for these chakras, but those points are related to their influence over our emotions, thoughts, and experiences in the material world. Again, just because they're not physical entities doesn't mean that they're not real.

Myth 3: Chakras are sources of energy.

Fact: Think of a river or a stream of water. We're using water as an analog for energy because flowing water is seen as a symbol of life and regeneration. There might be areas where this water forms pools or vortices. These pools aren't sources of water in themselves. For a stream to be considered fresh or clean, we want it to keep moving, right? If the water from this stream begins to stagnate in certain places, those places will soon become breeding grounds for all sorts of diseases.

Now, think of the nadis that act as energy pathways throughout the body. These pathways should always be kept clear and clean so that energy moves smoothly through them. When our chakras get blocked or stagnant, there's a chance that we'll experience all kinds of problems in our lives. Therefore, chakras don't produce energy but store them in a manner that ensures the health of our subtle bodies.

Myth 4: There are seven chakras in our subtle body.

Fact: Related to this myth is the one that believes that there's only one chakra system. Lets' address them one by one. First, we already know that chakras form at the meeting points of nadis. Now, these meeting points are 114 in number. This means that we have 114 chakras in our bodies. So why seven chakras, you ask? Well, according to the different schools of thought, two of these chakras have no corresponding physical basis. In other, only 112 chakras can be worked on.

Again, 112 is a huge number for us to be working on. So, these are divided into seven different classes, each with 16 different qualities. So, think of these seven chakras not as standalone energy centers, but rather as classifications for different kinds of energy. This classification doesn't exist on the metaphysical level, but it helps us understand the concepts more clearly. In yoga, these chakras are supposed to correspond to the seven different schools of yogic thought.

Now, when it comes to the chakra systems, we mostly talk about the seven-chakra system. Do you know that this is only one of the many different systems present? There are four-chakra systems, five-chakra systems, and so on. The seven-chakras system was popularized in the west by the book *The Serpent Power*, which was published by Sir John Woodroffe in 1919.

The good news is, every system agrees on three main energy centers—the sexual center, the heart center, and the head (or crown) center. This makes sense because all human beings experience their lives around these three centers. There's no need for you to get confused about which system is right. You can choose whichever system you want, as long as you understand what that means for your practice.

Myth 5: The seven chakras correspond to the seven colors of the rainbow.

Fact: When we trace the concept of chakras to their origins, we'll find that there's no description of the seven colors of the rainbow. Since chakras are conceptual, they're also described in conceptual terms. In some schools of thought, they're described without color. In others, they're described more poetically, for example, like the "color of a rain cloud." Also, since chakras are related to Hinduism, they originally feature different Hindu deities sitting on different lotuses. Now, these lotuses weren't always of one color. They usually had different shades and each shade symbolized something.

So, where did the rainbow concept come into the picture? In 1977, author and spiritual leader Christopher Hills published a book called *Nuclear Revolution*. This was the book that popularized the concept of the "rainbow body," which gave specific colors to each chakra. What does this mean for your practice? We need to understand that chakra healing works on the principles of visualization. Therefore, if you think that visualizing each chakra as a specific color helps you focus and enhances your practice, do so. This also means that you don't have to stay fixated on one color scheme or visualization pattern. In the beginning, you can follow some of the more popular concepts, but after some time, you can develop your ways of meditating on these chakras.

Myth 6: Each chakra corresponds to a particular psychological state.

Fact: If you've had even a cursory understanding of chakras from most of the books or articles available online, you might be surprised to come across this. After all, the basis of chakra healing is that it helps deal with different psychological and emotional issues that might occur when these chakras are blocked, right? Interestingly, this is not something that belonged to the original schools of thought. The reason for this is simple. In the original practice, chakras had nothing to do with the material plane. Or, more accurately, they saw this practice as one of transcending the material plane to find the spiritual one.

If you want to understand how this evolution occurred, think of how yoga has evolved over centuries to become a mainstay in western thought. There are so many different schools of yoga prevalent today in the west that it might be difficult to associate it with the original eastern traditions like Hinduism. In its original form, yoga comes from Sanskrit, where it means "to unify." In other words, the practice of yoga is based on the concept of Oneness. In most western traditions, there's a focus on duality, which yoga rejects. The ultimate aim of the practice is to merge our consciousness with that of the Universal Consciousness.

The same goes for chakras. The original concept of chakras is related to the process of self-actualization. This means a deeper knowledge of oneself, the Divine Energy within us, and how we can merge with the Divine Consciousness. This doesn't mean, however, that the chakras cannot help with mental and emotional health. The thing is, many western thinkers, psychologists, and spiritual leaders have been heavily influenced by eastern thought on their journeys. One of these people was the Swiss psychoanalyst and psychiatrist Carl Jung, who came up with these different psychological states that each chakra corresponds to. These classifications are a great way for us to understand how to use chakra healing to improve our psychological health, but the effect is more complex and nuanced than we might realize.

Myth 7: The main aim of chakra healing is to treat our physical (and other) illnesses.

Fact: This is related to the previous point. It's understandable that we first come to chakra healing when we feel like something's lacking in our lives, or when we suffer from issues that aren't entirely diagnosable or treatable through conventional methods. Even so, the purpose of chakra healing goes way beyond the material. You can think of it as a ladder or hierarchy of sorts. If you have to achieve spiritual health, you need to become a healthy vessel first. In other words, your physical fitness might be essential for self-actualization, but it's certainly not the primary aim.

Another way of thinking about this is that when we learn to balance our energies, we automatically improve our mental, physical, and psychological health. So it's more like a happy product than the main benefit. Again, this doesn't mean that you cannot use chakra healing to improve your physical, mental, and emotional health. There are only two main things to keep in mind. One is that your health depends on several complex and interrelated factors, which means you need to make the necessary changes in your lifestyle, take the help of your doctors, and also pay attention to the changes that occur in your body when you undertake this journey. You shouldn't blindly follow anything that is taught to you and be prepared to research and question wherever needed.

Two, the potential that chakra healing carries isn't restricted to physical or mental health. As important as these are, your imagination is the limit when it comes to chakra healing and working with energy. Therefore, don't be afraid of having lofty goals, even if it will realistically take you a long time to make those possible.

Myth 8: Chakra healing is an easy and quick solution to your problems.

Fact: When we're looking for solutions, and especially if we've been looking for a while, it can be tempting to believe that chakra healing will act as a one-stop solution to all our problems. Since chakra healing is primarily a spiritual undertaking, you need to understand that it will be neither easy nor quick. Even the most experienced practitioners of yoga and meditation take years before their practice yields results. Of course, what they're looking for might be much more complex than what you're seeking right now.

Even so, you cannot rush the process. The reason why chakras can be imbalanced, or why they create such a profound effect on our lives, is that they hold within themselves years (and even lives) of trauma and pain. When we begin any spiritual work, we should know that it isn't easy to rid ourselves of all these traumas. Some of them might be easier to heal from than others. That being said, you need to do a lot of work before you can consider yourself completely healed.

There's another reason why you shouldn't rush this process. Sometimes, when our wounds are too deep, we might seek a spiritual practitioner to help us on our journey. If we don't have patience, we might either expect them to solve our problems immediately, or we might end up signing up for courses or shelling money for sessions that promise miraculous results. The third reason for dispelling this myth once and for all is that chakra healing isn't exactly a finite process. If you think that going through this process once will cure you of all your issues and your chakras will stay balanced forever, you're mistaken.

If you think of a pipe or conduit, don't you need to periodically check for blockage and clean it regularly? The same goes for our energy pathways. Many things might happen in our lives that can lead to our energy centers getting imbalanced or blocked. Or, we might simply want to move on to a higher level of our spiritual journey. Chakra cleaning is an ongoing, even lifelong, process. It doesn't have to be cumbersome, however. Once you're aware of the steps you need to take to keep your chakras balanced, you can create your routine.

Just as physical and mental health go beyond diets, fads, and simplistic solutions, so too do chakra health go beyond a few sessions. More than anything, it's a way of life and a different way of looking at yourself.

Myth 9: Your chakras need to always be "open."

Fact: Since this is a concept that has gained a lot of momentum among spiritual healers, you might keep hearing that your chakras should always be open. This isn't entirely accurate. Let's go back to the example of a conduit. While you don't want it to be blocked or shut, you also don't want it to be overflowing with water, do you? If there's more water pressure in the conduit, there's a chance that it will burst. In the same way, we don't want our energies to be muted, but we also don't want them to be overactive. This can be disruptive rather than healing for us. This is why a better term for this is "balance." When our chakras are balanced, they ensure our physical, mental, emotional, and spiritual health.

These are some of the most prevalent myths around chakras and chakra healing. Now that we have a clearer idea of this concept, let's go through the seven chakras (according to the system we'll be following) and understand what they signify. Remember, even if these concepts come from different eras and diverse schools of thought, they ultimately help you gain a better understanding of yourself.

A Deeper Understanding of the Seven Chakras

In this section, we'll understand each of the seven chakras and their functions in our lives. We'll also get a better understanding of how we can use this knowledge to our benefit.

First Chakra: Root Chakra (Muladhara)

This chakra is located at the base of our spine. Physically, it affects different parts of our body, such as our nails, teeth, bladder, bones, kidneys, prostrate, lower digestive system, sexual organs, and excretory system. The element that represents this chakra is earth, and the color most associated with it is red. Symbolically, it's represented by a lotus with four petals, within which is a square. Inside the square is a triangle that faces downward. This figure is said to represent the birth of consciousness in human beings.

Since this is the first chakra, it deals with the most basic things that all of us need in life. Therefore, this chakra deals with our feelings of security, stability, self-sufficiency, and self-worth. All of us need certain things to survive. This includes food, water, basic clothing, housing needs, and a sense of security. Since our survival response is closely related to the fight-or-flight response that occurs when we feel stressed or threatened, the root chakra is responsible for this as well.

Second Chakra: Sacral Chakra (Swadhishthana)

This chakra is located about four fingers below the navel in our lower abdomen. Physically, this chakra is said to affect our sexual organs, kidney, pancreas, spleen, liver, stomach, gallbladder, upper intestines, lymphatic system, and autoimmune system. It represents the water element. The color associated with it is orange. Symbolically, the sacral chakra is represented by six petals of the lotus, along with a crescent moon and numerous circles. Both the circles and the crescent moon signify the cycles of life, death, and rebirth.

In Hinduism, being caught in this cycle is seen as the primary cause of all our misery and suffering. As long as you have karma to clear, you're going to be reincarnated on earth. This is why our greatest spiritual achievement is when we attain *nirvana*, which is freedom from these cycles. This is why the six lotus petals refer to all the negative aspects of human nature that need to be overcome to attain nirvana. This chakra is related to our sexual, sensual, emotional, and creative desires. Therefore, it affects our sexuality, personal relationships, relationship with pleasure, and self-worth.

Third Chakra: Solar Plexus Chakra (Manipura)

This chakra is located between the bottom of the rib cage and the navel. Physically, it affects the stomach, liver, gallbladder, kidney, middle spine, and small intestines. It represents the fire element and is associated with the color yellow. Symbolically, it's represented by 10 petals of a lotus, which contain within themselves an inverted triangle. While the triangle signifies the kundalini energy, the petals refer to the 10 negative aspects that need to be overcome to awaken this energy (and inner strength) within us.

Simply put, this is the seat of your power. This means that it's inextricably linked to your ego, which isn't necessarily a bad thing. When we think of an egoistic person, we tend to associate negative qualities like pride, anger, and aggression with them. Indeed, an inflated sense of ego doesn't benefit anyone; however, a healthy sense of ego helps with our self-esteem. It also helps us get a better grasp on our emotions, and gives us a sense of belonging in this world. When channeled in healthy energy from this chakra can help us manifest our dreams and goals.

Fourth Chakra: Heart Chakra (Anahata)

As is evident by its name, the heart chakra is located in the heart region. Physically, this chakra has a strong effect on our heart, lungs, diaphragm, arms and hands, shoulders, breasts, thymus gland, circulatory system, and rib cage. The element it represents is air, and the color associated with it is green (sometimes pink). Symbolically, the heart chakra is represented by a 12-petalled lotus, within which are two intersecting triangles—one upright and the other inverted.

The 12 petals here refer to the 12 beautiful qualities of our hearts. The symbol that is formed by the intersection of the two triangles is also known as a *yantra* (vehicle for a deity). These yantras act as aids in meditation as well. Spiritually, the two triangles are supposed to represent the masculine and feminine energies, the physical and spiritual realms, and the yin and yang energies. This means that the heart chakra stands for the balance between these seemingly opposite energies. This is also noteworthy because the heart chakra is seen as a bridge between the "lower" and "higher" chakras.

Not surprisingly, the heart chakra deals with matters of the heart. It's related to compassion, unconditional love, and meaningful relationships with ourselves and others. As such, it influences both our social and personal connections in this world and enriches our lives.

Fifth Chakra: Throat Chakra (Vishuddha)

The throat chakra is located in the neck and shoulder region, specifically at the base of our throat. It affects our arms, hands, neck and shoulders, teeth, mouth, gums, esophagus, vocal cords, trachea, throat, thyroid gland, and parathyroid gland. The element associated with it is ether or space (and sometimes, sound). The color most people relate it with is blue. Symbolically, this chakra represents a lotus with 16 petals, within which is an inverted triangle, which in turn holds a circle within itself. The entire figure represents spiritual growth.

The fifth chakra is seen as the first chakra that represents a more spiritual side of the chakra healing journey. Before you embark on such a journey, you need to cleanse your mind, body, and soul. Without a pure vessel, you won't reach anywhere. Thus, this symbol tells us that the necessary purification process has begun.

The throat chakra is the seat of intentional, healthy, and powerful communication. It's connected to the sacral chakra because that chakra is essential to our emotional and creative health. If our emotions are balanced, and if we're able to express ourselves clearly, we unlock our creative powers. At the same time, we also improve our relationships with ourselves and others. After all, good communication is at the heart of strong relationships. Out in the world, our throat chakra helps us in being our authentic selves. If we can be truthful to ourselves at all times, and if we have faith in ourselves and others, we become powerful in the way we present ourselves to the world. In other words, a balanced throat chakra helps us realize who we truly are, and helps us stay faithful to our truest selves.

Sixth Chakra: Third Eye Chakra (Ajna)

This chakra is located between the eyebrows, at a point that is referred to as our "third eye." Physically, it affects our eyes, ears, nose, brain, neurological system, pituitary gland, and pineal gland. In terms of color, it's usually represented by indigo. However, when it comes to the element it represents, there are some conflicting theories. Some spiritual teachers believe that the third eye chakra can be represented by light. Others believe that there's no element (that we know of) that can represent this chakra.

This is primarily because this chakra is seen as holding the secrets of the unseen world. The third eye is said to help us perceive things that the ordinary senses cannot. It's also said that the Universal Consciousness travels to the point where the third eye resides, which is why most spiritual seekers are asked to meditate at that point. We'll go into some detail about this chakra later, where we shall see why it isn't often associated with elements (or even colors).

Symbolically, the third eye is represented by two lotus people and a circle between them. The circle holds an inverted triangle within itself. These are seen as symbols of wisdom and awareness. In other words, they hold the secrets necessary for unlocking our spiritual journey.

This chakra is seen as the seat of self-awareness, intelligence, intuition, insight, concentration, and clairvoyance. First, it helps us gain a deeper understanding of ourselves. It helps us go beyond surface-level knowledge of ourselves and the world around us. Second, it helps us improve our concentration levels and attention span. Third, it sharpens our intuition and extrasensory perception. Those who want to attain spiritual enlightenment and nirvana usually meditate on the third-eye chakra for long periods and believe that, with practice, third-eye chakra meditation can even help us overcome our karma. Once we're free of our karmic baggage, we can sense true liberation.

Seventh Chakra: Crown Chakra (Sahasrara)

The crown chakra is the last chakra of this chakra system. It's located at the top of our heads. Physically, it affects the brain, cerebral cortex, pineal gland, nervous system, and endocrine system. The color associated with this chakra is either violet or white. When it comes to the element, most people agree that no element can represent this chakra. Symbolically, the chakra is represented by a 1000-petalled lotus containing an inverted triangle within it. This is supposed to represent the merging of our consciousness with the Divine Consciousness.

The sharpening of intuition that begins with the third eye chakra gets accelerated with this chakra. This is supposed to be the culmination of our spiritual journey, with enlightenment and knowledge flooding us. Those of us who have been seeking a connection with the Divine finally enter into the Union with energy. During this stage, we move beyond all the illusions that keep us from seeing ourselves and the world.

We understand that the barriers we've placed on people and things aren't real. We see that everyone and everything is connected. This realization brings with it inner peace, joy, and unconditional love for everyone. At this level, we finally achieve complete integration of our bodies, minds, and souls.

We now have a basic understanding of each chakra and the symbols associated with them. Before we move on to the benefits of balancing our chakras, let's understand the potential of kundalini energy.

Chapter 3
An Introduction to Kundalini Energy

Remember our discussion on the sushumna nadi? This is the central nadi that is essential to a spiritual awakening in human beings. However, this nadi remains dormant for most of us. This is the pathway that goes from the root chakra to the crown chakra, connecting all the chakras along its path. More importantly, it provides the path for the *kundalini* to awaken and rise throughout your subtle body.

If you've been interested in eastern spiritual traditions, you'll likely have come across this term. Even in western yoga circles, this term has become mainstream. This doesn't mean, however, that most people truly understand what kundalini means or how it can affect our lives. Before we begin, let me emphasize that this is a very powerful energy that shouldn't be trifled with. If you don't understand it, or if you use it improperly, you might end up doing more harm than good to yourself.

Let's understand this energy in greater detail in this chapter.

What Is Kundalini?

In Sanskrit, the word kundalini means "she who is coiled." Symbolically, the kundalini is depicted as a coiled serpent that lies dormant at the base of our spine. Remember the vital life force we've been talking about throughout the book? Well, kundalini provides energy to this life force. As such, it's seen as the ultimate source of creativity, intuition, and spirituality. Traditionally, it's treated as a Divine Feminine energy (Shakti).

Do all of us possess this energy? Yes. You might wonder, if this energy is so powerful and useful, why does it stay unawakened in most of us? What can we do to awaken it? Also, should we even awaken it in the first place? To answer these questions, we need to go deeper. When we experience consciousness in ourselves, it cannot be separated from thought. After all, we think, feel, and perceive things, therefore we exist. The ultimate aim for anyone who is on a spiritual journey is to witness Universal Consciousness. This is the consciousness that exists beyond thought and perception. Needless to say, this isn't something that everyone can, or should, experience.

The kundalini provides the energy needed for the prana to move through the chakras. This is when the chakras want us to reach a higher level of consciousness. This can only happen when we achieve sustained concentration. Just as the sushumna nadi doesn't get activated when we're going about our daily lives, so too the kundalini remains dormant when we're following our regular routines.

Since we're completely immersed in the physical and material world, it's difficult for our consciousness to detach itself from this world. Only when we leave the physical plane (through a meditative trance or a similar phenomenon) can we begin to tap into the potential of the kundalini. When this serpent-like energy moves from the base of the spine and reaches the crown of the head, it triggers a spiritual awakening that can transform us on the physical, mental, and emotional levels.

When this kundalini moves through the spine, it brings all our chakras into balance and helps us reach a state of pure bliss, joy, and love. In ancient times, the knowledge and practice of working with kundalini were restricted to a few spiritual masters. Now, this practice has become popularized in the west. It's believed that the first time a spiritual master achieved kundalini awakening within themselves, they went into a state of *samadhi*. What is this state of samadhi?

According to Hindu and Buddhist meditation practices, this is the highest state that a meditator can reach. At this stage, the practitioner remains attached to their physical body (thus, not leaving the physical plane) while reaching the highest level of meditation or concentration. At this level, they become aware of the Divine Consciousness, thus becoming aware of their true selves.

Once this state is received, the kundalini becomes awakened. Now, even after this serpent has come back to its original place at the base of the spine, this practitioner can awaken it when needed to experience a heightened sense of awareness.

How Does A Kundalini Awakening Occur?

When we come across a phenomenon that can have a profound effect on our lives, it's understandable that we want to initiate one within ourselves as well. The question is, is it safe or advisable to do so? How does a kundalini awakening occur in the first place? For most people, kundalini awakening can only occur after years of sustained spiritual practice, which includes meditation, pranayama, and yoga. The most important branch of yoga that helps in achieving this state is known as *hatha* yoga, which works to preserve our prana. This is why many spiritual teachers practice kundalini yoga and also help others learn it.

That being said, a kundalini awakening can also be an extremely spontaneous process. This means that, if our subtle bodies are ready, the kundalini can awaken and balance our chakras on its own. How is this possible? Well, when we speak of detaching ourselves from the physical world, we don't necessarily mean that you need to give up on this world or retreat to a remote place in the Himalayas. Of course, where there's solitude, you have a greater chance of getting in touch with your inner self, which aids in this process. The aim, however, is to become one with your true nature. This can only happen when you don't let the world affect you too deeply, even as you participate in it.

So, instead of doing something special, all we need to do is ready our minds and bodies to become awakened. When the kundalini recognizes that we're ready, it'll move through our chakras and trigger an awakening.

Benefits of Kundalini Awakening

A kundalini awakening is an intense, powerful, and rare experience. The first thing you need to understand is that kundalini awakenings aren't as common as they're made out to be. In the original context, practitioners needed to prepare for months and even years before they could experience something of this level. Even though people go through spiritual awakenings (which are extremely powerful in their own right), not all of these are kundalini awakenings.

That being said, a kundalini awakening has the power to change not only your life but also your perception of yourself. It's impossible to come out of this experience and go back to your life as it once was. Here are some of the benefits can a kundalini awakening can bestow on your life

- A kundalini awakening is a spiritual awakening (though all spiritual awakenings are not kundalini awakenings). This means that it gives you deeper insight into your true nature and helps you come face-to-face with your potential. It's the peak of your self-actualization journey in many ways.

- After a kundalini awakening, you'll feel a deep level of spiritual connection with everyone and everything in the world. Since this is a journey toward oneness, you won't differentiate between the different entities you meet. You'll understand that everything is connected and that all our thoughts, actions, and experiences have a profound impact on one another. This can help you recover from the usual feelings of anxiety and helplessness that you feel when moving through the world. You start believing that no one is at the mercy of another. Each of us has the power to create and shift reality if we want.

- When you feel connected with everything around you, you naturally feel an increased sense of compassion and empathy toward others. Not only will you want to spend more time in nature, deciphering the language of trees, animals, and other beings, but you'll also look for meaningful relationships in the human world. This doesn't mean that you'll look down on certain relationships or people. On the contrary, you'll see the potential for love and meaning in every connection.

- You'll unlock the powers of your mind and intellect. Not only will your creativity be enhanced, but your intuitive and psychic abilities might also become sharpened. Now, this isn't a magical phenomenon by any means. Each of us possesses the ability to connect deeply with ourselves and others. After a spiritual awakening, these abilities come to the fore. This is why after such an experience, many people start working as intuitives, healers, and spiritual guides. This way, they help others achieve their spiritual (and other) goals in their lives.

- After a kundalini awakening, you'll find yourself experiencing pure bliss. Don't confuse this for having a stagnant life, however. As balanced as you might feel within yourself, this awakening might act as a wake-up call for you to change whatever is not working in your life. You might find yourself questioning your relationships, your career path, and the decisions you've made so far in your life. You might not change everything (though many people do make significant changes in many aspects of their lives), but you'll certainly not take things for granted. In this way, it might even be an uncomfortable period in your life, and the lives of your loved ones. Everything that you have so far accepted as a given in your life might need a second look.

Issues Related to Kundalini Awakening

Of late, there have been instances of people getting scared of kundalini awakening. There are numerous reasons for this. One, people don't always understand the context in which these experiences occur. This doesn't mean that people in the west cannot have such experiences, just that it's important to understand the process fully before committing to it. Two, this is a process that, if attempted deliberately, should be done under the guidance of an experienced and credible spiritual teacher.

While most spiritual processes can be initiated ourselves, this isn't one of them. To understand this, let's understand another process that has recently become very popular in the west.

Once more, there has been an exponential growth in the number of retreats that offer ayahuasca experiences, or adventures that require you to ingest psychedelic plants. The thing is, such experiences are native to the Indigenous peoples in the Amazon basin. They're the ones who know how to ingest these plants, what to do before and after ingesting them, and the reason behind undergoing this process.

In other words, they have a natural and deep connection with these vines, which has a profound impact on their regular lives and spiritual experiences. They might have different reasons for undergoing these processes than we do. When such experiences are replicated in western settings, it's important to make sure that the *shaman* or spiritual leader who is leading the session is well-informed and understands the nuances of the situation.

What happens when this is not the case? People suffer from "bad trips" and psychotic breaks that don't only ruin the awakening process for them but can also have deeply negative impacts on their material lives.

Three, it's important to be ready. The same situation can be greatly beneficial to one person, while simultaneously being destructive to another. The difference lies in whether they've prepared themselves physically, mentally, and emotionally for this experience. Again, going back to the mystical experiences that people might have while ingesting ayahuasca, some people might have amazing spiritual experiences that change their lives for the better, while others might have such a destabilizing experience that they swear off anything like this in the future. In this era of instant gratification, it can be difficult to understand the importance of patience, discipline, and perseverance required when seeking out this experience.

Four, and this is related to the last point, make sure you're mentally and emotionally able to withstand this experience. At best, this can be an unpredictable experience for even healthy people. At worst, it can cause mental and emotional havoc for someone who is susceptible. For example, you might come out of this experience with the ability to heal your past wounds and trauma. You might also get reminded of your traumas in such a way that it leads to greater depression and confusion. Again, the answer lies in adequate preparation. This also includes having the right support from friends and family, and if needed, a professional. If you're in the middle of this awakening process and cannot seem to cope with the changes that are occurring within you, you will need support from others to stabilize yourself. This is especially true if you face or have faced stressful situations regularly or have had a traumatic past.

This section isn't meant to scare you. On the contrary, I want to emphasize that the kundalini is a Divine Feminine presence that is nurturing, intuitive, and creative. It's not forceful or destructive in itself. The force lies with us, and herein lies the crux of this discussion. Whether you're preparing for an awakening or not, you should not force this experience on yourself. We need to respect this energy and understand that it seeks out those who're ready and able to undertake this journey. When you force this awakening, the energy might not even travel through the sushumna nadi as it should. It might rise rather rapidly and uncontrollably in such a way that it begins to move through the ida and pingala nadis. When this powerful energy goes sideways instead of straight, it can cause permanent damage to you mentally and physically.

So, allow the process to unfold at its own pace. In the meanwhile, get closer to the person you want to be and the life you want to lead, both materially and spiritually.

Symptoms of Kundalini Awakening

There are many symptoms of a kundalini awakening that you can look out for. It's usually a combination of these symptoms that can tell you if you're experiencing this or not. Sometimes, you might experience some of the less usual symptoms as well. A good spiritual teacher can certainly help in determining whether you're being awakened. Remember, if you experience any of the more "destructive" or "unsettling" symptoms, you can always ask for help. In most cases, there's nothing to be afraid of as long as you have faith in the process. Here are some of the symptoms you might experience during this process:

- You feel more connected than ever to everyone, especially the Divine. This will include a feeling of pure bliss and unconditional joy.

- Your abilities get developed or you suddenly exhibit abilities you didn't know you had. For example, your intuition becomes much sharper than before, which allows you to understand what is real and what is not. You can sense things that other people cannot. You're more finely tuned into other people's emotions and energies.

- You also develop the ability to truly understand your life and your past experiences. For example, you might be more open to digging deeper into your past traumas to understand how your life has turned out this way. Or, you might gain a better understanding of how your mind works, thus gaining the confidence to use it for your good. This goes beyond the intellect that helps us navigate the material world. You might even begin to understand the true nature of reality during this process.

- If old traumas resurface, you might find it easier to work through them. One of the major elements of a spiritual awakening is that you can work through blocks and traumas in a way that was not possible before. I'm not saying that it will become extremely easy to navigate them, but it will become possible. You will gain the strength needed to go through the required process for healing your issues.

- You will feel like you're having a conversation with the universe. This might happen in the form of signs and synchronicities (for example, seeing repeating numbers or specific symbols regularly). You might feel like you're a part of meaningful "coincidences." You might also receive important information (for your soul) from angels, guides, and other cosmic entities. In other words, you'll feel like you're always at the right place at the right time, listening to the right words.

- This is a time of immense, and often, lasting change. The universe will keep giving you signals to change your life. You'll find yourself unable to ignore the areas of your life that need special attention. Even if you feel uncomfortable at times, it'll be impossible for your life to stay the same as it was before this awakening. The good news is, you'll also possess the strength and confidence needed to make these changes. Some of them might be small, others might be bigger, but all these changes will have a profound impact on your future.

- A spiritual awakening of any kind essentially begins with ego death. Remember we talked about how our ego can protect us in the material world? Well, it does so by creating walls or layers that keep our deepest fears, insecurities, and desires hidden from us. It's said that if we begin to know who we truly are, we might not be able to handle it at first. So, in a way, our ego protects us, but at a great cost to our true selves. If we want to fulfill our true destiny, we have to meet ourselves, which means that these walls and defenses need to go, This, in effect, is an ego death. Now, ego death isn't a "bad" experience by any means, but it can be extremely uncomfortable and unsettling for most of us. Without these defenses, we might even end up feeling extremely exposed and vulnerable to this world.

- This can also be a time of strange visions, vivid dreams, and other phenomena that cannot be easily explained. These aren't symptoms that everyone experiences, but you might. For example, some people report that they suddenly start seeing snakes everywhere or begin dreaming of them regularly. Since the kundalini is represented by a serpent, this is seen as a strong indicator of such an awakening. Similarly, some people might begin to have strange visual and auditory sensations, have out-of-body experiences, and have strange cravings that they've never had before (for example, craving food at midnight or craving different foods than those you're used to).

- This is also a time when your mind and body react in a very different way than usual. For example, you might find yourself experiencing spontaneous bursts of energy where anything seems possible. You might also experience phases when you feel extremely fatigued and unable to do anything. Some of this might be a part of a normal spiritual awakening process. Since this is an intense experience, you can expect to feel these dips in energy now and then. Similarly, you might also feel some physical symptoms that are uncomfortable, such as gastric, autoimmune, or throat-related issues. It's important to note that whenever you experience a negative physical symptom that's persistent, you should get yourself checked by a medical professional. Don't self-diagnose and self-medicate, and don't hide behind the idea of awakening. If the doctor rules out any actual medical issues, you might investigate further to understand if something else is going on.

- If your kundalini is trying to rise but you haven't worked on your chakras properly, chances are, the energy will get blocked. This blocked energy can manifest in certain concerning ways in your body. For example, you might struggle to sleep properly (or at all). Or, you might experience intense heat in your spine. Some people also experience involuntary shaking of their bodies. These symptoms can alarm you, but you need to understand that this is a result of blocked or unbalanced chakras. Work on balancing your chakras so that your kundalini finds a clear path for its ascent.

- This can be a period of intense (and unexpected) pleasure and pain. For example, some people experience physical and sensual pleasure in their bodies. Similarly, there are periods when you might feel extremely buoyant and euphoric. Other times, you might feel intense sensations of grief that have no discernible reason being them. One of the reasons for this is that you're opening yourself up to this world. This brings with it pleasure and pain in ways that you didn't know were possible. It also means that you might respond to the world more deeply than ever. For example, when the world was going through a pandemic, there was a lot of grief and suffering in this world. Even if you were relatively safe and secure, you might find yourself absorbing these energies from around you. If you're going through a kundalini awakening, this capacity becomes even more intense.

Should You Try to Initiate a Kundalini Awakening?

The short answer is no. Since this is an experience that we still don't know everything about, we should be careful before deliberately initiating it within ourselves. More importantly, when we seek out a particular experience, we create a layer of resistance between us and that experience. This is why many spiritual teachers tell us that the best (and most difficult) thing to do is to reach a state of flow. In this state, we simply exist and let the experience happen to us. We shouldn't confuse this with a state of defeat or fatalism. The more accurate term here would be "surrender."

We should prepare our minds and bodies for such an experience, without getting obsessed with it. Even during the experience, the most effective way to deal with the intense experiences is to allow them to happen. The more we resist or fight against the emotions or thoughts that surface during this time, the more difficult the process will get. So, we can look at some practices that you can do in your daily lives so that your body and mind become adequate vessels for change.

In any case, you'll be creating a positive impact on your own life, which is more than enough reason to go through this process. Some of the things you can do are

- **Practice mindfulness and meditation:** These practices can help you become more present and increase your concentration. As you become more aware of the world around you and within you, you'll be ready to welcome deeper insights into your soul. These are amazing practices to keep in mind when you're going through a kundalini awakening as well, as they will help calm you down and focus your energy where needed. In the beginning, even short periods spent meditating can help you immensely.

- **Practice yoga, breathwork, and pranayama:** All these practices will make it easier for your vital life force to move smoothly through the chakras. You might opt for a particular kind of yoga or a few pranayama techniques for more focused practice, but almost all techniques will help you on this journey. If possible, choose a credible and skilled teacher, especially in the beginning. Since you're working with your prana, you wouldn't want to mess with your energy through wrong poses, or poses that are executed improperly. Once you've gained confidence, you can start your regular practice.

- **Use music and dance to aid you on your journey:** Sound and music can help us on our spiritual journey. The same goes for dance. You don't have to be adept at singing and dancing, you just need to immerse yourself in these joyful acts. You can use chanting bowls, mantras, and music to help balance your chakras, especially your throat chakra.

- **Practice chakra healing:** In the upcoming chapters, we'll discuss the many ways in which we can keep our chakras balanced. When these chakras are aligned, it becomes easier for us to experience a spiritual awakening of any kind.

- **Practice love and gratitude whenever you can:** One of the simplest ways to open your heart and soul to a spiritual awakening, and to improve your life, is to intentionally cultivate a sense of love and gratitude in your life. There are times in our lives when we can feel love and gratitude without trying. Other times, it can be difficult to see beyond the pain and suffering and count our blessings. If you can send love, kindness, and gratitude to others during dark times, you've made it much easier for yourself to ascend spiritually in your life. After all, the ultimate aim is to feel unconditional joy and love for everyone, right?

Now that we've understood kundalini energy in some detail, let's understand the problems that might arise if our chakras are blocked.

Chapter 4
The Effects of Imbalanced Chakras on Your Life

All of us have phases when we feel tired, off-balance, or unwell. Depending on our medical history, environment, and lifestyle, we can get sick more or less frequently than others. As always, it's advisable to get regular medical check-ups done that give you a clear picture of your physical health. One of the reasons why you feel more unwell or tired than usual could be the imbalance in your chakras. We already know that chakras help carry our vital life force through the subtle body, which has an impact on our mental, physical, emotional, and spiritual health.

The good news is, we can carry out regular checks to understand if our health has been affected by chakra imbalances. In this chapter, we'll discuss in detail the areas of our life that are affected by chakras, and how an imbalance of chakras can create havoc in that particular area. Once we know this, we'll be better equipped to heal ourselves on all levels.

How Do You Know If Your Chakras Are Imbalanced?

Before we go into detail regarding each chakra, let's understand how we can direct our attention toward chakra imbalances in general. After all, most of us are not primed to think of our chakras the moment we start feeling "off." Indeed, a lot of this practice depends on cultivating our intuition to the point where we can understand our body, mind, and soul deeply.

If you're not used to thinking in terms of chakras and energy, but you've been feeling fatigued or "weird" for no discernible reason, the first thing I'd suggest is starting a journaling practice. Please don't worry if you haven't kept a journal in your life. You might think that this is another investment of your rather limited time and energy into something that might or might not show results. To this, I would like to say that journaling is an easy but powerful practice. You don't have to be a writer to keep a journal.

Think about it this way. Each day, we go through so many things that affect us, but after some days we forget those things. This is good in the sense that we shouldn't hold on to negative experiences. However, the problem is that our bodies and minds do hold on to those energies. When we forget things on the surface, but our bodies, minds, and spirits register them, they begin to affect our energies deeply and insidiously.

Journaling helps us become aware of these shifts in a more intentional manner. You can choose whichever form or structure makes the most sense to you when journaling. All you need to do is take note of the good and bad feelings, experiences, and thoughts that occur during the day. When you do this, you'll also make note of certain times when you felt tired, angry, or stressed. These emotions might emanate from real experiences, or they might be sudden and unexpected.

Once you get used to this, you can also note down your general routine (for example, your diet and exercise patterns), the environment in which you live and work (including the kind of people you meet, and any notable interactions you might have with them), and any situations or events that are notable to you. This could be something as huge as the pandemic and the changes that come with it, or it could be something good (like a promotion or a move) that is causing unexpected anxiety.

In the beginning, you might have to remind yourself to journal, but after a while, it'll become a part of your routine. Most people who've journaled for a long time see it as an ongoing conversation with themselves. This process will affect you in two ways. First, you'll gain an intimate understanding of yourself. Writing is a powerful act. Not only does it help you in noting down your ideas, but it also helps generate ideas and insights while you write. This can be transformative. Once you understand how you react to certain environments and changes, you'll understand what you truly need to feel balanced and whole.

Second, when we write things down in a journal and come back to them later, we begin to notice certain patterns that we might have missed out on otherwise. For example, if you find yourself feeling angry and stressed for no reason one day, you might dismiss it. However, if you see that your extreme emotions tend to resurface more frequently than they should, you might need to start examining them more deeply. Why are you feeling so angry? What are the general conditions that might be contributing to this feeling? Is there anything unresolved in your past that you need to work through? You will be able to ask, and then answer, crucial questions such as these.

Once you've gotten into a habit of journaling, you can refer to a small checklist that helps you understand if something's wrong.

- The first question is simple but profound. "Am I feeling off?" If you've worked on developing your intuition, you'll be able to sense this more quickly than most people. Sometimes, we don't realize that something's wrong until it's too late. Just as you should be conducting regular check-ins when it comes to your physical, mental, and emotional health, you should also be checking in with yourself energetically. So, if you're feeling too fatigued or lethargic (and your physical test results are okay), you might be suffering from a chakra imbalance.

- The second question is, "Am I falling sick frequently or intensely?" If you have good immunity in general, it might be concerning when you start falling sick too much. The same goes for inexplicable pain or numbness in certain areas of your body. Again, always consult with your doctor first to know if there's any underlying concern that needs to be addressed.

- The third question is trickier. Remember we talked about how chakras don't need to be *too* open? The thing is that our chakras don't work in isolation. If one chakra isn't working properly or is too blocked, there's a chance that another chakra might become overactive. This isn't a good thing. For example, if our sacral chakra is blocked, we might be suffering from low sexual and creative energy. However, if it's overactive, we might have too much sexual and creative energy, which can seem almost manic to us and others. For a system that craves balance, too much of a good thing is almost as bad as too little. So, ask yourself, "Am I feeling unusually energetic or manic?"

- Another great way to understand if your chakras are off-balance is to look at your performance and relationships at work. "Am I able to focus on the important things?" "How am I dealing with my relationships at work?" "What kind of an image am I portraying to others?" "Am I lacking in confidence and self-worth, or am I coming across as too aggressive and egoistic?" "Am I making too many errors, or am I repeating the same errors?" These questions can help you understand if your work is being hampered by imbalances in your chakras.

- The next one is related to your intimate relationships. "How am I showing up in my relationships?" "Am I giving too much or too little of myself?" "Do I suffer from trust issues, or am I gullible when it comes to people I love?" "Do I have healthy boundaries with my loved ones?" "Do I obsess over the relationships in my life?" "Am I feeling disconnected from my loved ones?" "Am I overly defensive or aggressive during conflicts with my partner, children, or parents?" Our emotional responses can help us understand if we're dealing with imbalanced chakras.

- Ask yourself if you have a specific reason for your chakras to become imbalanced. For example, have you recently gone through something devastating? Have you lost someone close to you, been a part of an accident or upsetting event, or dealt with extreme stress in your personal and/or professional life? In the last few years, it would be extremely normal for most people to have imbalanced chakras. Of course, some would be experiencing greater imbalance than others. The good news is, if we work on keeping our chakras balanced, they become resilient to shocks in their system. This means that they will bounce back and start working well much sooner than usual.

- Our root chakra is the chakra that forms the basis for how other chakras behave. Without a strong foundation, it's difficult for the higher chakras to function properly. Since this chakra deals with stability and security, any imbalance in this chakra can lead to feelings of extreme stress and even panic. This is also the chakra responsible for our fight-or-flight response. This response is inherently a protective mechanism that lets our body and mind know that danger is imminent, thus helping us prepare for it. Now, when this response is triggered daily, it can lead to repeated (and unnecessary) stress that doesn't help us. People who suffer from anxiety, stress, and panic disorders might need to work on balancing their root chakras. If you're feeling more stressed or anxious than usual, you might need to do the same.

- Last but not least, ask yourself, "Am I feeling in control of my life and emotions?" No one feels in control of their lives all the time. That being said, a certain degree of control means that we have the confidence to handle whatever we face in life. It also means that we feel like the creators of our destiny. There is a difference between surrender and defeat when it comes to our spiritual journey. When we're in control of our lives (in a balanced way), we're comfortable doing our job and surrendering the results to the universe. When we feel like everything's falling apart, or that we're a spectator to our lives, something might be wrong. On the flip side, if we become too controlling, it might indicate that we don't have faith in ourselves and our guides. If you have trouble letting go or going with the flow of things, you might have issues with your chakras.

There may be other symptoms that let you know if your chakras need attention. One thing that you should keep in mind is that it's almost impossible for your chakras to remain balanced at all times. So, don't get obsessed with the idea of balancing them every hour or every day. As long as you regularly check in with yourself, and make the required changes in your lifestyle, you should be fine.

Let's now look at each chakra in detail.

Imbalance in the Root Chakra

The root chakra is concerned with the earth element and is connected to our feelings of safety, stability, and security. When this chakra is imbalanced, we might have to deal with a host of physical and psychological problems. Physically, you might experience either too much pain or stiffness in your legs and feet, or you might feel that they're unstable. In other words, you might struggle to feel grounded physically. This can also result in knee pain, arthritis, sciatica, as well as issues with your bladder and digestive system. In males, it might manifest as issues in the reproductive system and prostate.

Psychologically, an imbalance in this chakra means that we're governed by extreme fear and insecurity. Since we don't feel assured about our basic needs, we might overthink and worry too much. During this time, you feel anxious about your survival, which means that you'll likely suffer from low self-esteem issues as well. Since our basic needs include food, which serves as both fuel and comfort for us, any imbalance in this chakra can also lead to eating disorders. When you combine feelings of insecurity with the need to provide yourself with extra comfort, there might be changes in your relationship with food.

Also, the root chakra is related to our family of origin. When we're feeling secure, we also feel assured of our relationships with our family members, and we feel safe at home. Most of us look at home as a place where we can just rest and recharge, and be our true selves. When our root chakra becomes imbalanced, we might feel uncomfortable at home, or we might not get the stability and security we receive from our family.

The overarching block that we might face in the root chakra is "fear."

Imbalance in the Sacral Chakra

The sacral chakra is associated with the water element. Physically, it's primarily related to our hips, lower back, and sexual organs. So, a blocked sacral chakra shows up in the form of pain in the lower back and hips, as well as with issues in our reproductive and sexual organs. Also, since this is related to our lymphatic system (water element), we can have issues related to our kidneys, bladder, and any other areas that deal with fluids. For women, there can also be issues with our hormones and menstrual processes.

Psychologically, an imbalance in this chakra manifests in the form of issues with our sexuality, creativity, intimacy, and self-worth. Do you feel emotionally disconnected from people you care about? Do you feel overwhelmed emotionally and need lots of time to yourself just to feel balanced again? Are you trying to close yourself off from anything that might make you feel intensely? Are you trying to blame others for your emotional responses? Chances are, you're dealing with an imbalanced sacral chakra. During this time, your creativity will also suffer. You might find yourself struggling to come up with good, imaginative ideas.

Since this chakra is related to our sexual energy, this might be a confusing time for us. Some of us might feel like our libido is in overdrive. Others might feel extremely shy and unable to express their sexual needs to their partners. We might also begin to act manipulatively to get what we want. When our sacral chakra is balanced, we have a healthy relationship with our sexuality. This means that we maintain a balance between our emotional and sexual needs, and focus on pleasure without getting obsessed with it.

In an imbalanced chakra, the overriding block is that of "guilt."

Imbalance in the Solar Plexus Chakra

The solar plexus chakra is related to the fire element. It's also the seat of self-esteem and personal power. A balanced solar plexus chakra means that you have a healthy relationship with yourself, you believe in your potential and do whatever it takes to fulfill it, and you also show confidence while dealing with others. It can most commonly manifest itself at work because we derive a large part of our identity through work.

Physically, this chakra is related to the abdomen, the middle of your back, and your sides. So, an imbalance can manifest in the form of digestive and abdominal issues such as gas, ulcers, and nausea, as well as eating disorders, diabetes, and low blood pressure. Psychologically, this is the time when we lose our sense of self. In some cases, we might become too timid and shirk responsibilities. We might shy away from leadership positions or anything that might hold us accountable. If we're already in a leadership position, we might end up doing a bad job in terms of decision-making. In general, we might be fearful of committing to anything or anyone during this period.

On the flip side, we might suffer from an inflated sense of self. We might become egoistic, arrogant, and judgmental. Since we inherently fear rejection at this time, we might overcompensate for it by becoming aggressive and even hostile in our interactions with others (especially our coworkers). We can also overcompensate for our sense of inadequacy by acting like perfectionists and effectively, not getting any real work done.

Since an imbalanced chakra affects our self-esteem, the main block of the solar plexus chakra is "shame."

Imbalance in the Heart Chakra

The heart chakra is related to the air element. Physically, it's related to our shoulders, arms, upper back, hands, heart, and chest. An imbalanced heart chakra will therefore manifest as pain in either of these areas, especially in the chest and upper back. It can also show up as extremely stiff or extremely flexible shoulders. If there's too much imbalance, it can show up as asthma and lung diseases, and heart conditions.

Psychologically, an imbalanced heart chakra means that we're unable to give and receive love in any form. When we talk of love, we mean self-love, love in our relationships, and compassion and kindness toward people in general. So, we might fail to love ourselves first. This means that we can be insecure about our value to others, or we might think that we don't deserve love at all. If someone does offer love to us, we might reject them because we don't truly believe that anyone can love us.

Sometimes, we might even be giving too much of ourselves in relationships, without being able to maintain healthy boundaries. Or, we might keep showing up in relationships where we're not getting anything in return. During this time, we might even suffer from feelings of jealousy, obsession, and codependence.

In other words, it can be really difficult for us to connect with others in healthy ways, which can make us feel isolated and lonely even in relationships. Since this is the chakra that can connect two different worlds, any imbalance in this chakra affects our ability to connect with others, leading to a lack of compassion and empathy and an overabundance of despair. Without love, it's difficult to see the value of life.

This is why the main block of this chakra is "grief."

Imbalance in the Throat Chakra

The throat chakra is associated with the space or ether element. Physically, it affects our throat, mouth, jaw, neck, and ears. Therefore, an imbalanced chakra can cause sore throat, laryngitis, issues with the thyroid, stiff neck and upper back, gum and tooth diseases, mouth ulcers, and hearing issues.

Psychologically, the throat chakra is the seat of clear and confident communication and authentic self-expression. If a balanced throat chakra means that you're a good listener, an imbalanced one means that you either don't listen at all, or you listen without any compassion. It also means that you shy away from public speaking, or talking to people in general. Since you have no confidence in your communication abilities, you might be too quiet and give up on opportunities to connect with people. You might also struggle to find your voice in another way.

When we know who we are and how we want to communicate with the world, we can get involved in creative endeavors that enrich us as well as others. With a blocked throat chakra, it becomes difficult to do so. So, your creativity is hampered. Since you don't have much faith in who you are, or you're trying to present a different version of yourself than your true self, you will have issues related to self-worth.

This lack of authenticity also means that we can become glib with words. If we're not too reserved, we might end up on the other extreme where we're the only ones doing the talking. Also, the quality of our words might suffer. We might indulge a lot in gossip and malicious discussions. When we're disconnected from our true selves, we can have trouble making decisions. Our weak willpower, coupled with our low sense of self-worth, can also make us prone to addiction disorders.

As this is the seat of authenticity, the greatest block in our throat chakra is "dishonesty."

Imbalance in the Third Eye Chakra

There's no element usually attached to the third eye chakra. However, it affects our vision, hearing, and brain. This is where our intuition and insight reside. When this chakra is imbalanced, it can lead to issues such as headaches, brain fog, nightmares, blindness or eye-related issues, deafness, seizures, and learning disabilities.

Now, when any of our chakras are imbalanced, we face anxiety issues. For example, if we don't feel secure or stable, we tend to feel anxious. Similarly, when we cannot express ourselves properly, we'll have anxiety or stress. One of the biggest blocks, however, comes from a block in our third eye chakra. Why is that? Well, when our third eye is balanced, we have a clear picture of ourselves as well as the world. We understand the reality on a much deeper level, and we connect with our truest selves. In the absence of all this, we don't know what and who to believe. Our sense of judgment suffers, and we might even lose touch with reality.

Mentally, we might suffer from issues with concentration and memory, and feel like we're often confused. We might be prone to making mistakes even with tasks that we've been doing for a long time. Due to an imbalance in this chakra, we might be feeling uninspired. Conversely, we might even feel like our imagination is overactive and even destructive. Since we don't know what the truth is anymore, we might become fearful of reality itself. We might overcompensate for it by behaving like we know everything there's to know about the world and beyond. Or, we might begin to distance ourselves from people who can show us the truth. In our bid to escape reality, we might even become prone to addictions.

Since this is the seat of clarity and insight, the greatest block to this chakra is "illusion."

Imbalance in the Crown Chakra

The crown chakra does not have an element attached to it. This is the chakra that connects all other chakras. Just as the root chakra can form the foundation on which other chakras are worked, so too can the crown chakra affect all the other chakras. This is the chakra that is associated with enlightenment and connectedness. Physically, an imbalance in this chakra manifests in the form of extreme sensitivity to sound and light. This can cause migraines and nightmares as well. It can also lead to learning disabilities and chronic fatigue.

Psychologically, we can face a whole host of issues when it comes to a blocked crown chakra. We can become prone to mental illnesses including delusions because of our loosened grip on reality. When our crown chakra is aligned, we feel connected to everything and everyone in the world, which makes us open-minded, receptive, and humble. We see our place in the world and understand that everything happens for a reason. Even in moments of grief, we can be patient.

In case of an imbalance, we become disconnected from the spiritual world. We might also become extremely materialistic. Also, we might suffer from narrow-mindedness and skepticism. Without faith, there's room for doubt and fear to grow to an extent where we lose empathy for other human beings. If you've become overly focused on yourself and your needs, and have become less accepting of others, you might be dealing with an imbalance in your crown chakra. When you're disconnected from yourself and your place in the world, you also lose your sense of identity and purpose. A balanced crown chakra helps us detach from the material aspects of the world while practicing compassion toward all living beings.

The biggest block to the crown chakra comes from "material attachment."

Now that we know how imbalances in each of the chakras can affect us, we can begin to work on balancing these chakras and fulfilling our spiritual destinies.

Chapter 5
Giving Your Inner Self The Things It Needs Most

On any given day, we're trying to juggle numerous responsibilities toward ourselves and others. We need to take care of our physical and mental health, and also make sure that the kids and elderly people in our families are taken care of. If we're dealing with physical, mental, and emotional issues, we have to make sure that they're handled before things get out of hand. At the same time, we cannot let other areas of our life suffer because of our struggles. Most of us spend a major portion of our lives trying to balance these disparate but interconnected aspects.

Only when these basic things are taken care of can we dedicate ourselves to discovering our purpose in life, staying true to it, tending to our passions, getting intimate with our true selves, and finding a community of people that nourishes and supports us. It's understandable, then, that our inner self tends to get ignored in this chaos. After all, most of us barely have time to work on the material aspects of our lives. How can we be expected to nurture our spirits as well?

In this chapter, I hope to offer you some relief. If you're reading this book, chances are, you want to embark on a spiritual journey, or at least be in touch with your inner self. However, when we're beginning this journey, we can feel rather overwhelmed. Here, we'll look at some of the things you can keep in mind when you start. We'll also go through the numerous benefits of chakra healing in living a truly balanced and healthy life.

Getting to Know Yourself

The first step on this journey is getting to know who you truly are. This isn't an easy question or one that can be answered in a few short sessions. However, there are certain questions that you can ask yourself to get a better understanding of yourself. Feel free to add more questions that are relevant to you.

- What are my core values and beliefs in life? You may have a lot of values, but some are essential to your existence. These are the values that you will do anything to defend. When things get difficult, you will go back to these values and stay true to them. For example, if you think that spending time with your family is of utmost importance to you, you will keep it above everything else. If your work commitments require you to stay away from your family for extended periods, you'll rethink those commitments. Similarly, if following your passion is of utmost importance to you, all the sacrifices that you have to make in doing so will seem worth it. These values will unite your personal, professional, and spiritual lives. Once you know what these values are, you'll have a clearer picture of what you stand for.

- What brings you the utmost joy? This might sound like a simple question because many things bring us happiness and pleasure. However, I'm talking about joy right now. How is it different, you ask? Well, happiness and pleasure are usually superficial and self-serving. I don't mean to say that there's a negative aspect to them. You can be happy about amazing things. The problem is, happiness is fickle. The moment you face an issue, your happiness will be threatened. Joy, on the other hand, comes from a deeper and purer place. It's usually connected to others in that we find joy in the community, in a sense of belonging, and in helping other people. Also, joy is related to our sense of purpose. Most people believe that suffering is best avoided, and I understand that. No one likes suffering, but the truth is that you cannot avoid suffering as long as you're alive. So, what you need to do is to make sure that you're not suffering needlessly. If you have a strong sense of purpose, it will make you resilient. Then, even amidst obstacles and hardships, you can find your capacity for joy.

- What are the events or memories that upset you? What brings you sadness, guilt, shame, anger, and despair? Are you prone to feeling angry or guilty more regularly than you should? Why? Is there any particular reason why you tend to exhibit certain emotions? I would avoid using the word "negative" here because one of the biggest issues we have in dealing with emotions is that we tend to attach judgment to them. For example, if we're feeling angry about the way our boss behaves with us, that's okay. We shouldn't behave destructively or lash out without thinking of the consequences, but feeling emotion isn't a bad thing. These emotions tell us something about ourselves, our pasts, and our inner lives. We should listen to them for clues into our psyche. When we layer guilt on top of our anger, not only do we keep ourselves from understanding ourselves, but we also make it more difficult to overcome the emotion. So, think of the more uncomfortable emotions that you face and try to understand why you might face them.

- What is your relationship with bare space? With silence? This is an uncomfortable question for anyone who is immersed in the material world. After all, the world we live in is so chaotic and crazy that we're used to the din that constantly surrounds us. If we're not dealing with the noise of people around us, we need to deal with the digital clutter that has become a permanent fixture in our lives. Our brains are always overloaded with (often unnecessary) information. So much so, that our relationship with sleep, rest, and relaxation has been forever altered. Ask yourself if you're comfortable sitting in silence for 5-10 minutes. Can you stay without your digital devices for an hour or two? Do you get proper sleep every day? What do you do when you have to time off for yourself? Do you fill your free time with more activities, or do you prefer to stay alone with your thoughts for some time? What do you think of doing nothing for some time each day? These questions will let you know how comfortable you are with the idea of silent contemplation. A lot of spiritual work is done in silence and honesty. As it turns out, you cannot be honest with yourself unless you face difficult questions in silence.

- What are your goals in life? When you're thinking about these goals, don't hesitate to think big. These goals can be related to your physical health, mental and emotional well-being, material abundance, relationships, and self-actualization. Create a vision of the person you want to be and the steps that will be needed to become that person. You should also make a list of your inherent strengths that will help you on this journey, as well as the challenges you might face. I would suggest that you create a mix of goals that are "big picture" in nature and those that are more specific and time-bound. For example, you can tell yourself that you want to include more joy in your life. In concrete terms, this could include taking up a hobby that nourishes your soul, meeting new people who resonate with you, and trying to do something for society. Based on your circumstances, you can look for ways in which you can achieve a part of these goals in the next few years.

- Are there any parts of your life that you want to improve? Do you have any negative cycles that you want to break free of? Do you have certain destructive thought patterns that you don't want to give your energy to anymore? Are there any behaviors that you think might be holding you back from reaching your highest potential? This could be related to your physical health, such as eating healthily or getting more exercise in your routine. Or, it could be related to your relationships. For example, you might have a tendency to disrespect your own and others' boundaries in your intimate relationships. Or, you might have trust issues that overshadow every relationship in your life. Only when you know where your blindspots are can you begin to work on them.

- What does a spiritual life mean to you? You don't have to be religious to want a spiritual life for yourself. Spirituality is a personal and deep connection with your inner self. So, only you can understand what you need. Do you want to heal your "inner child?" If so, how? Do you understand the wounds that your inner child carries, and why these wounds are there? Are you willing to do the work required to heal yourself? Are you willing to be the presence that you might have been seeking outside of yourself so far? For example, if you deal with abandonment issues due to certain incidents in your childhood home, you might have trouble believing that anyone will stay in your life. The issue is, when we're exhibiting a lack of faith in others, we're betraying ourselves. Our abandonment issues might keep us from becoming intimate with others, but they might also prevent us from showing up for ourselves each day. This has far-reaching effects on our life. So, can you let go of the difficult behaviors for your own sake? What does it mean for you to achieve balance in your life? How does spirituality help you in creating that balance?

Now that you know what you truly need, you need to start working on nourishing your spiritual side through chakra balancing. Let's go over the benefits that chakra healing provides us with.

Benefits of Chakra Healing

In this section, we'll go over the general benefits of chakra healing that all of us can experience, no matter what stage of our spiritual journey we're in.

- It can help you improve your physical health and well-being. As we've seen in the last chapter, each chakra has an impact on certain parts of our physical body. For example, an imbalanced root chakra can affect our feet, whereas an imbalanced throat chakra affects our throat, neck, and shoulders. When we work on balancing these chakras, we also recover from the pain and stiffness we might be feeling in these areas. On the other hand, if these areas of our body become too flexible or unstable, they become prone to injury. Therefore, balanced chakras ensure that our physical body remains strong and healthy.

- If you know which chakras are imbalanced, you'll understand why you're behaving in a certain manner. For example, if you're someone who comes across as insecure in your relationships, you might have an imbalance in your root chakra. Similarly, if you've always feared speaking in public, you might have issues in your throat chakra. Without the knowledge of chakras, you might be resigned to your fate and believe that you will always have these "weaknesses." Now, you can actively work on your chakras to release these blocks and tap into your hidden strengths. Remember, your strengths and weaknesses are two sides of the same coin, and are related to the same chakra.

- Chakra healing works on your emotional health as well. Whenever our chakras are out of balance, they signal some deep traumas or issues we need to work on. For example, if you're suddenly feeling a lack of imagination, and are struggling to connect with your friends and family, there might be an issue with your sacral chakra. Now, healing your sacral chakra will not only improve your creativity and imagination but will also help you improve your intimate relationships. To do this, you'll have to delve deep into your past and behavioral and emotional patterns. Why is your sacral chakra blocked? Why do you have issues with your emotional, sexual, and creative side? Is this something that happens often? By working on your chakras, you're also letting go of years of conditioning. Of course, this will take time, but once you start doing the work, you'll trigger a transformation in your emotional life.

- Chakra healing gives you a deeper insight into yourself. As I've mentioned before, all of us are born with intuition, but we tend to ignore it in the material world. Some of us might be more intuitive than others, but it takes practice to listen to our intuition and follow it regularly. Remember, your inner voice will never lead you astray. The challenge lies in quieting down enough to be able to recognize our inner voice. Chakra healing, especially the clearing of the three higher chakras, helps immensely with that.

- When we go through the trials and tribulations of life, we inevitably store a lot of negative energy in our bodies. Each interaction that we have, each thought that crosses our minds, and each emotion that arises in us brings with it a transfer of energy. So, if we live in an environment that is toxic for us, our chakras store that toxic energy within themselves. If we have poor eating, sleeping, or exercising schedules, they impact not only our physical but also our subtle body. Similarly, if we live with an argumentative partner, there might be a lot of anger or resentment stored in the subtle body. These energies have a destabilizing effect on our chakras and our lives. So, by regularly cleansing and aligning our chakras, we expel this negative energy from our subtle bodies, allowing for fresh energy to flow through them.

- If you've been working on your dreams for a while, but have been coming up against roadblocks, you might be facing resistance from yourself. This can be tricky to understand in the beginning. After all, if you want to be successful at something, or if you want a loving relationship, why would you be the one who's coming in the way of these dreams? The thing is, we don't realize when our energy becomes an obstacle in our path. For example, you might crave a stable and loving relationship, but you might tend to hold on too tightly to your partner. This could lead to obsession, codependency, and a lack of boundaries in your relationship, which in turn leads to a blocked heart chakra. Remember that all our chakras are connected, so an imbalance in one chakra will affect another. So, when we begin to heal our chakras, our energies become constructive rather than destructive. Sometimes the best way to achieve our dreams is by getting out of our way.

- Most of us have a difficult relationship with money. We might feel that money isn't to be enjoyed, or we might be irresponsible in the way we spend money. We might also feel like we're stuck doing the job we hate or living the life we don't want to, simply for the sake of money. Just like our personal relationships, our relationship with money is also rooted in the experiences we've had in childhood. If we've grown up in a home where money was always tight, we might feel guilty about enjoying our hard-earned money, even if we're financially secure. Many of our issues with money emanate from our root chakra, as that is the chakra responsible for security and survival. When we work on healing our root chakra, we repair our relationship with money. Not only that, but if we heal our sacral and solar plexus chakra, we'll become powerful in our own right. This will reflect in the work we do, the positions we hold, and the money we earn. In other words, chakra healing can hold the key to financial abundance.

- Chakra healing is the path to joy and love. I've mentioned before that every spiritual journey culminates in unconditional love and bliss (even if it never truly ends). In the west, most people still believe that mastering the crown chakra results in peace. While that's part of it, it's not exactly the right term for the experience. According to spiritual leaders, the word that most closely describes this experience is "ecstasy." When we know ourselves fully, and when our consciousness merges with the Universal Consciousness, we open ourselves to unadulterated joy and love. This is an experience beyond right and wrong, black and white, and some say, even beyond color (more on this soon).

Now that we know how to give our inner self what it needs, let's go into the specific chakra balancing processes that we can practice.

Chapter 6
Learning How to Balance Your Chakras

In this chapter, we'll discuss the different ways in which we can balance our chakras. Before we do so, let's understand a little more regarding these chakras, which will help us in choosing the best practices for balancing them.

The first thing to understand is that, while we talk about higher and lower energy centers in our body, we shouldn't think that one center is more important than another. For example, when you're beginning your chakra healing journey, you might hear advice that says that you should focus on your higher chakras rather than your lower ones. Or, you might believe that the throat, third eye, and crown chakras are the ones that are crucial for spiritual development. This can be misleading. Even if you don't go sequentially from the root chakra to the crown chakra each time, you need to pay attention to whatever chakra needs alignment. There is another reason for this.

When we talk about balancing our chakras, we talk about focusing on the underlying issues that we might be facing related to them. Of course, if we're having issues with food, sleep, or security, we should focus on the blockages present in our root chakras. However, according to ancient teachings, we can only truly balance our chakras when we detach ourselves from the physical aspects of it. What does this mean? When we talk about food, sleep, personal power, sexuality, and so on, we usually discuss all this in material aspects (as that is the only aspect we truly understand). This is also why there's a common misconception that the best thing we can do for our chakras is to open them.

When a chakra is closed, there's repression of the attached emotional or physical state, so opening it will set things right. This, however, is not the case. When our energy goes into overdrive, we're still attached to the physical realm (even more so). So, the chakra that was dealing with food, sleep, and security is now even more concerned with the same. On the surface, this doesn't sound like an issue. On a spiritual and energetic level, this is a problem.

The Two Dimensions of Our Chakras

This is an important concept to understand. Each chakra in our subtle body has two dimensions—physical and spiritual. At the physical level, we look at how each chakra can be balanced to improve our material lives. For example, when we balance our sacral chakra, we improve our sexual health and sharpen our intuition and creativity. This isn't the end of the journey, however. If we can deepen our practice, we might be able to unlock the spiritual dimension of an otherwise material chakra. At this level, the same chakra will become free of its material aspects.

What this means is that, contrary to popular belief, we can use any chakra to help us ascend spiritually. The power comes not from the chakra itself, but from how we visualize it and meditate on it. This is also why the practices that we use for chakra healing have a deeper significance than we think.

When we talk of yoga, meditation, or pranayama, we sometimes focus too much on getting the mechanics right. Don't get me wrong. It's essential to do the postures and techniques correctly, but that's not the end of it. The true essence of these practices lies in being able to achieve complete stillness of the body, mind, and spirit. When we can do this, we'll detach ourselves from the material aspects of reality, which will open up the spiritual realm for us.

Spiritual gurus talk about this concept in terms of two different homes for our spirit. The terms used are *antar* kshetra and *bahya* kshetra. "Kshetra" means region or area, "antar" means inner, and "bahya" means outer (in Sanskrit). So, when we exist entirely on the material plane, we want to enjoy our lives, and gain benefits, but also take it easy. It's a place of rest for us. We might not be achieving something amazing in this place, but we're also conserving energy. This is the inner region, where most of us reside throughout our lives. Even during the chakra alignment process, we might choose to work on the material aspect of our lives, which takes up less energy but is also less rewarding spiritually.

If we want to, and with dedicated practice, we can access the outer realm, which takes up more energy but also transforms us spiritually. This is the realm in which we can access boundless joy, love, and bliss. So, the ultimate aim of chakra balancing is to free each chakra of its physical dimension. That being said, we should certainly start small.

The Path to Chakra Healing

In this book, we'll be laying stress on healing and balancing the first five chakras—that is, from the root to the throat chakra. While you might find online resources that talk about healing the remaining two chakras as well, we'll be discussing these because you're still a beginner when it comes to chakra healing. The last two chakras are almost entirely spiritually inclined. We need to attain mastery over the first five before we can be ready for them.

Another reason for this is that when it comes to the transition from the throat to the third eye chakra, there are very few concrete steps that you need to take to make it possible. We need to spend as much time in silent contemplation as possible so that our intuition is sharpened and we become aware of our inner lives. When it comes to the journey from the third eye to the crown chakra, there is no real step. Of course, you might find resources that ask you to perform certain meditations, visualizations, and yoga postures, and they might help. However, the real journey is one of surrender and unwavering faith in the Divine.

Practiced meditators and spiritual gurus advise that this is the part of the journey that cannot be forced (though I would argue that none of it should be). It's like walking into the dark with your eyes, assured that you will be protected and that you'll reach where you should. The only difference is, you're walking into the light and your eyes have never been as wide awake as now. Confusing? It can be, especially for beginners. When we come to this stage of our chakra healing journey, we will see that all the conventional wisdom we've gathered so far is turned on its head. Instead of doing more, we're doing less. Instead of making changes in the physical realm, we're staying still and waiting for the changes to occur within us. Instead of working with elements, we're working with nothingness. Instead of seeing "nothingness" as a negative or deficient quality, we're seeing it as an abundant one.

This is why many people believe that the last part of the journey should be done under the guidance of a spiritual teacher, if possible. In ancient eastern traditions, our gurus were the only ones we could trust because they would lead us to the Divine. For this book, we'll limit ourselves to the first five chakras, which you can align more or less on your own.

Methods for Balancing Your Chakras

In this section, we'll look at some of the most powerful methods that we can use to balance our chakras. Before we do that, let's understand how even small tweaks to our current lifestyle can have an impact on our chakras. We already know that our physical, mental, and emotional environment can play a huge role in the health of our chakras. Since chakras deal with energy, we need to understand their working in energetic terms. If we're experiencing an intense emotion (one with more energy or heat) such as anger or frustration, we need to look for ways to cool it down. Like, if our chakra imbalance causes us to become heated, we cannot eat hot or spicy food, or become more aggravated during this time. This will only upset the balance further.

During this time, we need to eat cooling foods, do something to cool down our body temperature, or simply spend some time in silence. This will bring our chakras back into balance sooner. In other words, our diet, sleep routines, and exercise routines also play a role in aligning our chakras. This is why most teachers emphasize the importance of clean eating and following a disciplined routine each day, even beyond the actual meditations, yoga postures, and other practices. Now, let's look at these practices in some detail.

Chakra Meditation and Visualization

Meditation is a powerful way to balance our chakras. Meditation is an ancient practice that originated in eastern religions like

Hinduism and Tibetan Buddhism. There are many different kinds of meditation that one can practice depending on what their goal is, but all of them deal with similar principles. Simply put, meditation is about focusing our attention on a particular thought, object, or feeling in a way that helps us master our emotions, improve our mental and physical health, and unlock higher realms of consciousness.

While master practitioners might meditate for several hours a day, you don't need to do that as a beginner. The good news is, even short periods of dedicated meditation practice can yield amazing results. I understand that the initial challenge is to train our minds to focus on one thing. It can seem a bit frustrating in the beginning, but after some time, it'll become easier to steady your mind and concentrate.

Another practice that can help you is mindfulness. This is a practice that asks us to focus entirely on the present moment. We don't need to specifically concentrate on anything, but we need to accept whatever thoughts and feelings come into our awareness during this time. Again, this is not easy because we're used to thinking either about the past or the future. When we learn to live in the present without judgment, we'll begin to align our chakras as well.

If we want to go a step further in our meditation practice, we can try chakra meditation, combined with visualization. How do we do this? We can focus on a chakra and its associated qualities and energies when we meditate. For example, we can combine a simple breathing meditation with a focused chakra meditation. In this, we can meditate on, say, the root chakra. When we meditate, we can focus on our basic needs, our home, and our sense of security. If there's something that's making us fearful or anxious, we can focus on breathing through that fear.

Another way in which we can do this is through visualization. Visualization is a technique in which we use an image to concentrate on. In the case of chakra meditation, we can either focus on the symbols associated with each chakra (discussed in the second chapter), or we can focus on any symbol that we want (such as a wheel or spinning disk). Since each chakra is related to a particular area of the body and is also associated with a particular color, we can also visualize using these images. For example, if we're dealing with the throat chakra, we can visualize a blue light emanating from the throat. Similarly, if we're dealing with the heart chakra, we can visualize a green light at that point. When we focus on this image with the intention of purifying and align the corresponding chakra, we can create powerful changes.

The Importance of Sound in Chakra Healing

The most powerful combination that can help us in aligning our chakras of sound, visualization, and meditation.

Mantra Meditation

Many people visualize the chakras according to the symbols associated with them. Within each symbol, a specific mantra is installed, which is known as the *bija* (Sanskrit for "seed") mantra for that chakra. In Hinduism, a bija mantra is a very powerful syllable or sound. These sounds have the energy of the Divine Consciousness or the universe within them. They vibrate at a unique high frequency which can be used to power your meditation practice.

There are two things to keep in mind when dealing with bija mantras in your chakra meditation. First, these bija mantras aren't specific to the chakra but to the element associated with each chakra. So, when we speak of "LAM," which is said to be the bija mantra for the root chakra, we're talking about the earth element which resonates with this sound. Why is this distinction important? See, each element comes with a specific property of its own. For example, water is connected to intuition and emotion (which is why the sacral chakra influences these qualities). Now, if we want, we can place these elements in different chakras. For example, we can place the earth element in the heart chakra simply by doing chakra meditations using the appropriate bija mantra. The question is, why would we want that?

We've seen that our chakras, and the energies they associate with, are more fluid than we think. This means that we have more power over our chakras than we would like to believe. If we tried to place the earth element in the heart chakra, what would happen? We would become more grounded in our relationships, right? This can be a healthy change of pace from the air element that's associated with our heart chakra. As a beginner, you might not want to do this as it might get confusing for you. Nevertheless, this is something to keep in mind for your future practice.

Second, the bija mantras are extremely powerful. Therefore, it's of utmost importance that you pronounce these mantras correctly and clearly. In the beginning, it's advisable to take the help of someone who knows how to do so. Let's now look at the corresponding bija mantras for each chakra:

- Root chakra—LAM

- Sacral chakra—VAM
- Solar plexus chakra—RAM
- Heart chakra—YAM
- Throat chakra—HAM
- Third eye chakra—OM
- Crown chakra—Silence (no mantra)

Binaural Beats Meditation

Certain meditation experts believe that adding binaural beats to our meditation routine can help us receive more benefits from our practice. What are binaural beats? It's an illusion that forms when we hear two different sounds having slightly different frequencies in both ears. For example, if in one ear you hear a sound with a frequency of 140 Hz, and in another, you hear a frequency of 130 Hz, your brain will process the difference between the two frequencies to make you hear a sound of (140-130) Hz or 10 Hz. This is known as a binaural beat.

There are three main conditions for a binaural beat to form. One, the difference between the frequencies should be less than or equal to 30Hz. Two, both sounds should have absolute frequencies less than 1000 Hz. And three, each ear has to listen to a different tone at the same time. Now that we know what binaural beats are, let's see how they can enhance our meditation practice. In general, experts believe that simply listening to binaural beats can create the same benefits as a meditation practice. This is because these beats make the brain work at the same frequency, and show the same signs, as it does when we meditate. As such, binaural beats have immense potential in helping us lower our stress levels and feel more relaxed, increase concentration, reduce anxiety and improve our moods, foster creativity, and even manage pain.

There is a range of binaural beats that can be used for specific purposes as well. For example, beats in the 1-4 Hz range (also known as the delta range) can help with relaxation and deep sleep. Those in the 4-8 Hz range (theta range) help to reduce anxiety, foster creativity, and boost our meditation practice. In the 8-13 Hz range (alpha range), these beats decrease anxiety, making us feel more relaxed and improving our mood. In the 14-30 Hz range (lower beta range), binaural beats help in improving our memory, concentration, and problem-solving abilities.

Even though research in this area is still in its nascent stage, there's enough promise for researchers to agree that binaural beats meditation can help with anxiety, stress, and concentration. If you're trying to incorporate this into your practice, you should make sure that the sounds aren't loud, nor should you go for prolonged exposure. This is simply so that it doesn't hurt your ears. Also, people with epilepsy should consult with their doctor before incorporating binaural beats into their routine.

Crystal Healing

Simply put, a crystal is a solid material in which all the atoms are arranged in an extremely ordered manner. Crystal healing is also something that has been a part of many eastern traditions. Again, let's back to the concept of energy. Our chakras get thrown out of balance when we absorb disruptive energy from our environment, both external and internal. It's believed that crystals possess certain properties and vibrational energies that make them effective in balancing our chakras.

Since crystals have energy, they naturally react with chakras to bring about changes in our subtle (and hence, material) body. Of course, this also means that every crystal either aligns with a certain chakra, is neutral to it, or has the potential to throw it off balance. When we use the right crystal for each chakra, not only do we help align our chakras and cleanse them of any negative energies they might be carrying, but we also reconnect with our truest selves. In other words, the right crystals can unlock our potential and help us live healthy and successful lives.

In some cases, the healing energy of these crystals can help us work through years of deep-seated trauma as well. Some people also believe that crystal healing helps manage their emotional health as well as physical pain. Of course, we need to know how to use these crystals for maximum benefit. There are four major ways in which we can use crystals for our chakra healing journey:

- We can use them to decorate our house strategically. This means that by placing these crystals in the right places, we can cleanse our space using them. When our environment becomes pure and healthy, it affects our chakras as well.

- We can also wear these crystals as jewelry. When these crystals come in direct contact with our skin, they transfer their power vibrations to our body, which has a healing effect on our chakras.

- We can sleep with these crystals by placing them under our pillows. This way, the vibrations get transferred to us in our subconscious state of mind.

- Meditating with crystals is one of the most common ways of tapping into their healing powers. You can either place the crystal on the area of your body that corresponds with the particular chakra, or you can use it for a visualization meditation. During meditation, you need to set your intention in such a way that it brings about healing in your subtle body. You can also chant mantras (including bija mantras) to boost your meditation practice.

An important thing to remember about crystals is that when we use them regularly for our benefit, we drain them of their natural energy. This makes them less effective over time. At the same time, since these stones have the power to absorb energy from their surroundings and us, they might start vibrating with negative energies from time to time. This is why it's important to keep our crystals cleansed, charged, and activated. There are a few ways in which we can do this.

To cleanse our crystals of negative energy, we can either soak them in salt water or place them under running water, for a minute. Placing them in sunlight for about 10-12 hours can also help purify them. You can also cleanse them by burning sage over them for about a minute, or by immersing them in a sound bath for 5-10 minutes. Certain crystals are powerful in cleansing other crystals of their negative vibrations. Some of these larger stones are selenite slabs, quartz clusters, and amethyst geodes. The smaller stones that have this ability include hematite, carnelian, and clear quartz. By placing the crystal in need of cleansing beside one of these stones for a day, we can make them fit for use again.

When the crystals are drained of energy, you can either give them a sound bath, immerse them in salt, bury them in the ground, burn herbs over them, place them under the full moon, or soak them in water that has been charged by the moonlight. You can also charge them using your breath or meditating with them to get the help of your spiritual guides. Once these crystals are charged, you can use them for your chakra healing activities. This will keep your chakras activated during practice.

Essential Oils for Chakra Healing

Essential oils are oils extracted from particular plants or herbs and used in aromatherapy. These oils are known to be extremely beneficial for chakra healing. First, there are certain oils (such as lavender) that are known to provide sleep benefits to people. Rubbing these oils on your pressure points also has the effect of alleviating stress and anxiety.

When it comes to chakra healing, the concept is similar to that of crystals. Since we believe that every plant has its vibrational frequency, it can be used to help clear blockages from our subtle body. Healers also believe that essential oils can rid our chakras of negative energies while simultaneously boosting the positive energies present in them.

There are many ways in which we can use essential oils for chakra healing. We can either spritz them in the atmosphere when we begin our meditation practice, or we can massage ourselves with them. We can also combine meditation, visualization, and prayer with the right essential oils for our chakra healing journey. In the next few chapters, we'll look into the specific essential oils that can help heal each chakra.

Before we do that, however, it's important to use essential oils safely. Even though you might have read something online, or you have a trusted teacher, it's always a good idea to do your research before applying essential oils to your skin. These oils can be quite potent, so have as much information as you can before working with them. Also, you should not apply these oils directly in their concentrated form. Learn how to use them with the appropriate carrier oils. Also, be aware of the appropriate dosage of these oils.

Before you apply these oils to your skin, always carry out a patch test on a small area. If there's any irritation, stop using them immediately. If you're using these oils for aromatherapy, make sure that everyone who inhales the diffused oils is safe from them. As a general rule, avoid using them with small babies or pregnant women around. Also, your pets might be allergic to or get harmed by, some of these oils. Only when you're sure of the effects of these oils on yourself and those around you, you could use them in your chakra healing practice. Now that we've understood the basics of chakra healing practices, let's look at the first five chakras and the healing practices that can help balance them.

Chapter 7
How to Heal Your Root Chakra

When our root chakra is balanced, we feel a sense of belonging and security. We feel grounded emotionally and physically, experience a surge of strength within us, and have a strong sense of self-worth. We have a strong and healthy digestive system, and we feel a sense of independence. If you've been feeling like your root chakra is blocked, here are some practices you can do to heal it.

Meditation Practice

For any chakra, you can practice different kinds of meditation and visualization. Before we begin any meditation practice, it's advisable to get into the flow of things using a simple breathing practice such as the "box breathing" meditation. The first thing to do is to sit with your spine straight in a quiet place. This could be anywhere that your mind is at ease. Since you're dealing with your subtle body, your spine should be straight so that your life force can flow easily through the sushumna nadi. At the same time, don't try to force yourself or unnaturally arch your back. Our spine has a gentle curvature which should be maintained.

After this, you can place your hands on your knees, preferably with your palms facing upward. Once you're comfortable, take a gentle breath through your nose and feel your belly move outward. You can keep your eyes open or closed, but try to concentrate on your breath. While you inhale, count to four.

After that, hold your breath gently for another count of four. Then, exhale through your mouth for another four counts. Finish this meditation by holding your breath for four counts. As you can see, your breaths make a box of "inhale-hold-exhale-hold." This will calm you down and prepare you for any chakra meditation that might come afterward. Remember, be gentle with your breath at all times. You don't need to force anything, and you're not in a hurry to reach anywhere.

Now, you're ready for your root chakra-specific meditations. Since the color associated with this chakra is red, you can combine a simple breathing exercise (alternating between gentle inhales and exhales) with your visualization of the color red. If you prefer, you can also visualize a red spinning disk or a red lotus (or any symbol that you find easy to concentrate on). Since we're trying to heal our root chakra, we can try to intensify the energy of the symbol we're trying to focus on. For example, if we're visualizing the color red, we can either imagine the color becoming stronger (in a gentle way), or the particular area (such as the base of our tailbone) filling up with red. Similarly, we can also imagine that the red disks are spinning freely and are full of energy, symbolizing that they're not stuck and imbalanced anymore.

We can also combine our meditation practice with the chanting of the bija mantra "LAM" as many times as we can. This will activate our root chakra and align it.

Grounding Practices

Since the root chakra is related to safety and stability, we can ground our energies in a few different ways to heal this chakra.

- Spend as much time as possible, doing activities such as walking, running, yoga, pilates, dance, hiking, and even gardening.

- Since our feet are affected deeply by our root chakra, we can do a simple practice to heal the root chakra. In this, we use any ball that we can roll using the soles of our feet. First, we take one foot and shift our weight on it to support ourselves. Then, with the other foot, we gently roll the ball for some time. We repeat this with the other foot. This gentle pressure will not only help relieve stress but will also help activate our root chakra. Even the simple act of walking barefoot (in a safe space) on the grass in the morning can have a healing effect on our root chakra.

- Sound baths are also a great way to ground yourself if your root chakra is out of balance.

Affirmations

A simple yet powerful way of inviting positive energy into our material and subtle bodies is by repeating certain affirmations to ourselves. Affirmations are any positive sentences or phrases that act like mantras or chants in a way. When we keep repeating these phrases with faith, we send energy to the universe regarding our intentions. The universe then responds with similarly positive energy. This is a great way of creating our reality.

When it comes to root chakra healing, we want to assure ourselves that we're safe, stable, and taken care of by the earth (our element). So, you can repeat a few affirmations like "I am safe," "All my basic needs are met," "I have a healthy relationship with money," "The earth takes care of me," "I am well-nourished and protected by the earth," and so on. You can address anything that makes you feel insecure and fearful by turning it into a positive affirmation. Of course, the key lies in believing your own words.

Yoga Practices

Yoga is one of the most powerful ways to align your chakras. Not only does it energize your chakras, but it also brings you closer to your true self. As a beginner, I would always suggest that you seek out an experienced teacher so that you can do the poses in the right manner. Some of the yoga poses that can help ground us are the bridge pose, warrior pose, mountain pose, standing forward pose, tree pose, and side-angle pose.

Crystal Healing

The stones that heal the root chakra are black or dark red. Their energies are protective and grounded in nature. If you're placing the crystals in your house, some of the areas are your bedroom or the center of your home for grounding purposes. If you want to place them there for protection, you can place them in the four corners of your home, or beside the front door. On your body, the best areas are your feet or groin area. Some of the crystals that are particularly powerful in cleansing our root chakra are

- bloodstone (grounding and power),
- hematite (cleansing),
- red jasper (grounding),
- red pyrope garnet (purification),
- black tourmaline (protection against negative energies),

- smoky quartz (grounding and cleansing), and
- black obsidian (protection and grounding).\

Essential Oils

Two main essential oils can specifically help with root chakra alignment.

- **Vetiver**—Also known as khus oil, this is an oil extracted from the khus plant that grows in India. This is a great oil to strengthen your mind and body connection. At the same time, it helps us feel grounded and accelerates our emotional growth.
- **Red spikenard**—This oil is great for stabilizing ourselves in our physical body, grounding us without diluting our energies, and gaining control of our lives.

In the next chapter, we'll discuss how to heal our sacral chakra.

Chapter 8
How to Heal Your Sacral Chakra

A balanced sacral chakra manifests itself in the form of high emotional intelligence, sharpened intuition, sexual, sensual, and emotional vitality, good humor, and compassion toward ourselves and others. In this chapter, we'll look at a variety of simple practices that can help heal our sacral chakra.

Once again, it's a great idea to focus on the element related to the chakra: water. We'll heal our relationship with water to align our sacral chakra.

Meditation Practice

The color associated with this chakra is orange, so we can use it to aid our chakra meditation and visualization practice. Since we're combining the color orange with the water element, a beautiful visualization practice we can do is of the sun setting over a body of water.

The first thing you need to do is sit in a manner that makes your sacral chakra region flexible, especially if you've been feeling stuck. To do this, first, relax the area around your hips and lower back, and then loosen your pelvic region through movement. Now, since we're using our body as a canvas for this visualization, let's place an orange sun in the sacral chakra region, below which is a body of water.

Now, as we breathe in, we see the gentle waves washing up on the shore as the sun begins to set on the horizon. On breathing out, the waves move back. You can see this act as a gentle cleansing of your sacral chakra, with the water removing any stuck or negative energy in this region.

When it comes to mantra meditation, the bija mantra used here is "VAM."

Healing Through Water

Water has a gentle and cleansing energy. It's also a symbol of intuition, emotions, creativity, and sexuality. So, you can use the healing sounds of the ocean or rain to aid your meditation practice. If you're fortunate enough to live close to a moving body of water (such as the sea or ocean, or stream), you can also spend some time in quiet reflection at these locations.

Another highly recommended practice connects the imagery of the moon to that of water. We already know that the moon has a deep relationship with water (as we can see in the form of tides). Now, in this meditation practice, you combine the bija mantra "VAM" with the healing effect of water in your sacral chakra region. For this, you need to sit in a comfortable position. Then, imagine that your sacral chakra region is filled with a white or silver moon. While visualizing this image, gently breathe in and out as you chant the corresponding bija mantra. You can do this for 10-20 minutes each day.

Affirmations

When we use affirmations, we focus on clearing any guilt or doubt we might have regarding our sexuality and creativity. For this, you can use simple mantras such as, "I feel safe and confident in expressing my sexuality," "I have faith in my sexuality, imagination, and emotions," and "I remove all guilt that might be blocking my sacral chakra."

Yoga Practices

The best yoga poses for healing your sacral chakra include the bound angle pose, garland pose, crow pose, triangle pose, and camel pose.

Crystal Healing

The crystals that help heal the sacral chakra usually have yellow or orange tones (and in some cases, blue-green). They aim to get us in touch with our emotional, intuitive, and feminine side. In the house, these crystals can be placed in an area where you do creative (or any) work. On your body, the best place to keep this crystal is in your pelvic area.

One of the most powerful crystals for working with the sacral chakra energy is the moonstone, especially the peach moonstone. This stone can connect us to the Divine Feminine energy within us and also sharpen our subconscious mind. It's also said to help with issues around fertility. Some of the other crystals that can help balance the sacral chakra are

- spessartine garnet (helps in kundalini awakening),
- citrine (for inviting pleasure and joy into our lives),
- carnelian (for creativity, vitality, and tapping into our hidden potential),
- imperial topaz (used for manifestation),
- autumn jasper (manifesting positivity and protecting our energy),

- tiger's eye (for courage and a healthier connection with our sexuality),
- peach selenite (for energy and peace),
- mookaite (for handling change positively),
- orange calcite (for passion), and
- apricot Botswana agate (for connecting to our earthly energy and gaining physical strength).

Essential Oils

The two main essential oils that can help align our sacral chakra are

- **Pink pepper seed:** This oil can help us heal any issues we might have regarding our sexuality. For example, if we suffer from low libido, or we have issues with our body image or self-worth, this oil can help us overcome them. It can also help us love ourselves and feel connected to our erotic side. Last but not least, it helps us overcome any guilt we might face while expressing our sexual desires.
- **Lavender:** This is an oil that can have a healing effect on any chakra. Since it's associated with a relaxed and sensual vibe, it can especially help heal our sacral chakra.

Some other oils that can help in sacral chakra healing include rose, galangal, jasmine, tangerine, patchouli, and sandalwood.

In the next chapter, we'll discuss ways of healing our solar plexus chakra.

Chapter 9
How to Heal Your Solar Plexus Chakra

A balanced solar plexus chakra ensures that we come in touch with our power. What does that look like? Well, you'll have the confidence to believe in your abilities, you won't need to be aggressive or defensive when dealing with other people, and you'll believe in your own choices. Physically, this also means that you'll have a healthy digestive system.

When you know who you are, you'll not waste your power on people or interactions that no longer serve you. You also won't be afraid of your potential and will seek out leadership roles for yourself. In this chapter, we'll learn how to heal our solar plexus chakra.

Meditation Practice

The solar plexus chakra deals with the color yellow, as well as with the fire element. This element energizes us from within and gives us the strength and courage needed to live up to our potential. The region of our body that is associated with this chakra is the abdomen. So, we'll incorporate all these elements in our meditation and visualization practice.

The first thing to do is to sit straight and focus your attention on your abdomen. If you're feeling out of balance in your solar plexus chakra, you'll likely have issues in your belly area. So, you can gently massage this area for some time so that this area gets stimulated positively. Once you do this, you can start inhaling and exhaling gently. As you inhale, your belly contracts. As you exhale, it becomes full. When you do this for some time, your body will generate heat through your breath, which will begin to align your solar plexus chakra.

You can also use the power of fire to burn down any negative emotions you might be feeling. Remember, this isn't to be used in a destructive or aggressive sense. All we want is for these gentle flames to remove any issues we might be struggling with.

You can also use bija mantra meditation for your solar plexus chakra, using the mantra "RAM."

Channeling the Power of the Sun

Both the sun and fire can be used to align our solar plexus chakra. Here, you can sit beside a fire to derive power from its heat. Some people also like doing rituals in which they write down their biggest obstacles or issues on a piece of paper and throw them into the fire. Of course, it's important to be safe whenever you're dealing with fire. Please don't do anything impulsive or aggressive around the fire.

Get as much sun as you possibly can. Again, this should be done healthily, and you should apply sunscreen to protect yourself from the harmful effects of sun exposure. That being said, the sun is a symbol of power like no other. Not only does healthy sun exposure increase our vitamin D levels (which can make us feel more vital and strong), but it can also help improve our mood and help counter stress and depression. As much as possible, limit your exposure to artificial light and fill your space with natural light.

Affirmations

The biggest block to the solar plexus chakra is a lack of personal power. Whether you've become timider or more aggressive than usual, the underlying issue is that you feel helpless when it comes to your own story. So, the aim is to reclaim your narrative. The first thing to do is to stop seeing yourself as a victim. I'm not suggesting that external circumstances have no role in your condition. However, if we become fixated on everything wrong in our environment or life, we'll never move ahead. So, take responsibility for the things that you can change and let go of those that you cannot.

Next, you need to release any anger that you might have kept inside you. Even if the anger or frustration isn't recent, it can corrode you from the inside and severely dilute your power. Developing a sense of humor can also help in making you feel more powerful in life. When we laugh at ourselves, we take away power from anyone or anything that threatens to disrupt our life.

Then, you need to examine everything in your life that might be holding you back. Once you know what these are, channel your willpower toward affirmations such as "I am strong, courageous, and responsible," "I can do anything I set my mind and heart to," "I have the power to make choices in my life," and "I am a whole person."

Yoga Practices

Some of the best yoga poses to channel your power are the sun salutation pose, boat pose, bow pose, sitting half-spinal twist, and warrior pose.

Crystal Healing

The crystals that help in healing our solar plexus chakra are usually bright yellow. When we need to place these crystals in our home, the best places are those where there's water, such as the bathroom or laundry room. On our body, the navel is the best area to place these crystals. Some of the best crystals for solar plexus chakra healing are

- citrine (abundance and optimism),
- yellow jade (reclaiming your narrative),
- yellow topaz (inner harmony and strong sense of self-worth),
- yellow sapphire (connecting to the knowledge and power bestowed on us by the Divine),
- yellow jasper (inner strength and clarity), and
- Golden tiger's eye (confidence and clarity).

Essential Oils

One of the most potent essential oils for healing our solar plexus chakra is black pepper oil. This oil helps us break free of the past patterns that have held us back. Many of our restrictive behaviors might have emanated from issues in the past, some of which we might not even be aware of. If we want to let go of the past and refresh our energies, this oil can help.

Other than this, you can also use cinnamon, rosemary, sandalwood, myrrh, clove, lemongrass, and atlas cedarwood for healing your solar plexus chakra.

In the next chapter, we'll discuss how to heal our heart chakra.

Chapter 10
How to Heal Your Heart Chakra

When our heart chakra is balanced, we're in a position to give and receive love. We're kind and compassionate not only with others but also toward ourselves. This has a positive impact on all our relationships. Also, since this chakra is said to connect the material and spiritual worlds, it can help in bringing balance to both areas of our life.

In this chapter, we'll discuss how to heal our heart chakra.

Meditation Practice

When our heart chakra is blocked, we feel lonely, misunderstood, and unloved. At times, we might also protect ourselves too tightly because we fear getting hurt. The element associated with the heart chakra is air, and the colors are green and pink. Let's combine them to create a soothing meditation practice for ourselves.

First, we make sure we're sitting straight. The heart chakra has an impact on our entire chest cavity, so make sure that this area doesn't feel deflated or restricted. Our lungs are supposed to protect our heart, so we need to channel the power of breathing in such a way that we feel strong enough to love again. So, the next thing we do is imagine our entire chest filling with emerald green light. This light tells us that we have nothing to be scared of.

After this, we visualize our heart as a pink light at the center of this chest cavity. This is our heart, which is soft but not weak. Now when we inhale and exhale deeply, we focus on this beautiful light that fills us with unconditional love and empathy for all human beings.

The bija mantra associated with the heart chakra is "YAM."

Learning to Love Again

The Sanskrit word for the heart chakra is "anahata," which translates to unhurt. This is what we want our heart to learn—the ability to love as if it has never been, nor can ever be, hurt. It does sound challenging, doesn't it? After all, to live is to love, and to love is to open yourself to the possibility of getting hurt. I'm not suggesting that you might never be betrayed in love after this. All I'm saying is that no one will have the power to take away your capacity for love anymore. What can be better than this?

The best thing to do for your heart chakra is to practice grace and gratitude whenever you can. When things get difficult, try to look for the things that you should be thankful for. Reach out to your loved ones and thank them for supporting you throughout your life. Even if it's not possible to say the words to those who need to hear them, keep a gratitude journal in which you can note down the smallest things that brighten your day. If the big problems can upset us, the small blessings can make things right.

Affirmations

You can also practice loving-kindness (*metta*) meditation to heal your heart chakra. This is a meditation that involves sending compassion and love to everyone around us. While focusing on your breath, you can chant affirmations that give you the strength to practice unconditional love. The first phase of this practice starts with sending a lot of love and healing energy toward yourself. You can use phrases like, "I am worthy of love," "I am a kind, loving, and compassionate being," or "I thank myself for all the love and support throughout my life."

Next, you turn these loving affirmations toward your loved ones. You think of the people who have taken care of you, your birth family as well as your chosen one, and anyone who has shared moments of love and laughter with you. Send positive energy toward them. After this, look for people who are relative (or total) strangers, but who improve your life in one way or another. Our lives are touched by many people daily, and we cannot survive without the generosity and warmth of strangers.

Think of the people who take care of your home or community, the friendly barista at the coffee shop you frequent, or the grocer who always greets you with a smile. These recollections will fill you with immense gratitude and love for people you don't even know. The last part of this exercise is the toughest one. During this phase, you need to visualize people who might have disappointed, hurt, or abandoned you.

Admittedly, this isn't something you can do in the beginning. That's okay. The good thing is, as you start practicing the first three parts of this meditation routine, your heart will open up to the possibility of forgiving the people who hurt you. Once you're able to do this, you'll have unlocked a whole new version of yourself.

Yoga Practices

Since we're looking at opening up our heart, we can practice any *asanas* (poses) that bend our bodies backward. Some of the poses you can try are the half-bridge pose, cobra pose, and upward-facing dog pose. You can also incorporate the camel pose and the wild thing pose into your routine. Remember, with any yoga pose, always take it easy and don't strain yourself too much. Your body might take some time to become as flexible as you want it to be, but it will happen. Be patient and listen to your body at all times.

Crystal Healing

Crystals that align the heart chakra have soft and rich vibes, signifying love and compassion. When placing these chakras in your home, look for a location that has meaning for you and your loved ones. It could be a space where all of you come together to eat, talk, or play. It could also be a space where you have fond memories with your children, partner, or parents. When placing the crystals on your body, focus on the heart. Some of the crystals that aid in heart chakra healing are

- green aventurine (opening your heart and being optimistic),
- rose quartz (compassion toward yourself and others, unconditional love),
- Malachite (positive transformation), and
- amazonite (Divine guidance toward love).

Essential Oils

Two of the most powerful essential oils for heart chakra healing are discussed below:

- **Pine:** If you want to release painful memories of the past, and begin healing from old wounds, this oil can help you. It can help us let go of things that have hurt us, even those that we haven't had closure from, and urge us to move forward with an open heart.

- **Rose:** Rose oil is considered by many as the best oil to heal your heart chakra. It can help us practice kindness, love, and compassion toward ourselves and others. It can also help us practice strength without becoming rigid or closed-off.

In the next chapter, we'll discuss how to heal our throat chakra.

Chapter 11
How to Heal Your Throat Chakra

When your throat chakra is balanced, you can communicate effectively with everyone around you. This means that you become a good and empathetic listener, as well as a compassionate and impactful speaker. Not only this, but you have the confidence to live your life exactly as you're meant to. You're not afraid to follow your true path, even if it means making difficult decisions and having uncomfortable conversations with those you love.

In this chapter, we'll discuss how to heal our throat chakra.

Meditation Practice

Our throat chakra affects our neck, throat, head, mouth, ears, teeth, and jaws. The color associated with it is blue, and the element is ether or space. When we begin to meditate on our throat chakra, we first need to get rid of any stuck energy around this area. First, we need to make sure that our neck is aligned with our spine at all times. Then, we need to do some neck stretches that will loosen our neck muscles. We can also loosen our jaws and get ready to heal our throat chakra. We can now imagine a blue gem or blue light at the center of the throat and breathe gently as we imagine this light healing our chakra.

The lion's roar is a meditation technique that specifically helps with throat chakra healing. First, you need to inhale gently through the nose. Then, you open your mouth and your eyes as widely as possible. After that, you will begin exhaling through the mouth. However, this time, you need to stick out your tongue and make a loud roaring sound while exhaling. Repeat as many times as you can.

This practice will allow you to get rid of any blocks that are keeping you from being your most authentic self.

The bija mantra associated with this chakra is "HAM," which we can combine with our visualization practice.

Meeting Your Authentic Self

Deep down, all of us know who we are. However, years of conditioning have distanced us from our true selves. Making the journey back to ourselves can be as challenging as it is liberating, so we need to get used to expressing ourselves authentically.

One of the most powerful ways to do this is through journaling. In your journal, write down your dreams and aspirations, even the wildest ones, even those that you've never said aloud to anyone. Make a list of the things that bring you joy. It doesn't matter if those things are lucrative or sensible; they just need to make sense to you. Also, think about your most important relationships, and ask yourself if you're sacrificing a part of yourself to keep those bonds alive. One, you might be holding on to someone or something simply because it's been a part of your life for a long time. Two, you might have something amazing with someone, but you're afraid to show your true self to them because you fear losing the relationship.

In both cases, you need to learn how to communicate with others in a way that your true self doesn't pay the price. When you're trying to heal your throat chakra, you also need to pay attention to your ears, because the kind of listener you often determine how you show up in your relationships. You cannot truly express yourself unless you've made a committed effort toward understanding others.

Affirmations

Some of the affirmations that can help heal your throat chakra are "I am my most authentic self," "I dare to express myself without diminishing the voice of others," "I am a creative being with the power to imagine whatever I want" and "My voice matters."

Yoga Practices

The most effective yoga poses for the throat chakra are the plow pose, fish pose, bridge pose, supported shoulder stand, and cat stretch.

Crystal Healing

The crystals that heal the throat chakra have a gentle, thoughtful, and free-flowing vibe. In the house, they can be placed in any area where you spend most of the time talking to the people in your life. This could be where you talk to your partner or children, or where you entertain guests. It could also be a place where you can express yourself freely, either through your artistic pursuits or through any activity that is meaningful to you. On your body, the crystals need to be placed on your throat. Some of the crystals that can help heal the throat chakra are

- aquamarine (for trust, authenticity, and going with the flow),
- blue topaz (clarity and honesty when it comes to your feelings),

- blue lace agate (enhanced communication and creativity), and
- angelite (to encourage you to be truthful to yourself and others).

Essential Oils

Two of the most effective essential oils for throat chakra healing are

- **Frankincense:** This is an oil that helps you become more receptive to the energies surrounding you. This increases your intuition and you're able to understand what exactly is going on in a particular situation. This, in turn, improves your communication because you can pick up on both verbal and non-verbal cues. Also, this oil can help you pause and decide on the best way to respond to difficult situations. It can make you calmer and keep you from reacting in a brash manner. In other words, it makes your communication more effective and empathetic.
- **Blue chamomile:** This oil can help strengthen our communication with the Divine. It can make it easier for us to hear what our guides want to tell us; in other words, it can help connect us to our inner voice.

In the last chapter, we'll briefly touch on some of the common mistakes you might be making as a beginner on a spiritual journey.

Chapter 12
Common Mistakes Made on The Healing Journey

When we're just beginning our chakra healing (and spiritual) journey, we might feel unsure of ourselves. This is to be expected. The spiritual path is one of faith, which means that we need to embrace uncertainty and believe in ourselves, especially when the going gets tough. As a beginner, you might worry that you're making a lot of mistakes. I'm here to tell you that that's okay. Even very experienced healers and spiritual teachers make mistakes.

Two main things separate experienced teachers from beginners. One, they have unshakeable faith in the Divine. So, they believe that when they make mistakes, their guides will be there to protect them. Two, they're humble. The more they know about the nature of reality and the spiritual path, the less they profess to know others. They don't become rigid about their beliefs; in fact, they're open to communication, dissent, and doubt. They don't take things personally and practice compassion at all times.

In this chapter, we'll briefly talk about some of the things you should keep in mind when working with energy.

Don't Rush, Don't Compare

The most important thing is that you shouldn't rush the process at any stage. No matter if you think you're ready, you need to be patient and wait for the signs that let you move on to the next stage of the journey. Also, like any other journey, the spiritual one derives its value from the experiences you have along the way. Even if your ultimate aim is enlightenment or salvation, you still need to savor each milestone that you achieve.

The same goes for comparisons. This is your unique journey. In the eyes of the Divine, no one's early, and no one's late. Everyone is moving at the pace that they're meant to. In the spiritual realm, time and space don't exist in the same way as they do in the material world. This also means that you're not a success or a failure in your spiritual journey. So, don't fixate on how far someone else seems to be on their journey. Focus on making your journey amazing.

Be Aware of the Energies in Your Environment

All of us are susceptible to the energies around us. This goes for experienced healers as well as beginners. Of course, experienced healers might be able to pick up these energies faster than you. Nevertheless, you should make it a point to always cleanse your space before working with energy. The energy in your environment can be affected by the disease, death, suffering, emotional angst, and so on. Your healing practice will suffer immensely if you don't refresh the energies you interact with.

Be Aware of, And Protect Your Energy

When you're just starting, you might not realize how much negative or problematic energy you might have stored within yourself. Even the most experienced teachers have energies that can come in the way of their spiritual journey. These energies are called "shadow energies." Just as you need to cleanse the space around you, you also need to make sure your shadow energies aren't interfering with your healing work.

Also, as you begin to ascend on your spiritual path, you might attract the energies of people who need help. Whether you choose to work as a healer or not, these interactions can drain your energy and leave you with nothing for yourself. The same goes for healing other people. If you're practicing reiki, say, you need to make sure that you don't end up taking on everyone's pain and illness without protecting yourself. This can be done by making an energy circuit using our hands so that there's no one-way transfer of negative energy to us.

Not Being True to Yourself

There are many different paths you can take on your spiritual journey. In the beginning, it can be tempting to focus on what others are doing, or trying to be a certain kind of healer. Not only will this not help you, but it will also keep you from becoming a true spiritual seeker. The whole aim of the process is to become intimate with your true self. This means that you have to pay attention to your unique gifts and abilities. Only when you understand why you've been chosen for this path will you be able to help yourself and others.

A spiritual journey is as demanding as it's rewarding. What's the point of facing this journey as anyone but yourself?

Conclusion

Many people believe that no one chooses a spiritual path for themselves. The path chooses you. It doesn't matter if you're the most "rational" or "materialistic" person around, if you're meant to follow a spiritual calling, you'll have no choice in the matter. At the same time, there's nothing as powerful as human will, so if you've come this far on your journey, you've made a choice.

When I was beginning my healing journey, I was confused, lost, and perpetually tired. I didn't know what to do, whether I was doing too much or too little, and if I was even going in the right direction. I understand that part of the process is related to hearing our voice amidst the din. Still, I didn't expect to feel this overwhelming. This wasn't even the worst part of the process. More than anything else, I feel desperately lonely on this journey. I knew there were others on this journey; I even had the opportunity to be guided by some amazing teachers. Nevertheless, because the nature of this journey is internal, it can sometimes feel like you're the only one on this path.

Fortunately, I was able to see enough signs and rewards that kept me going. I often wondered, though, what if I didn't have patience? What if it took a bit longer for any kind of results to show? What if I felt like giving up even before I had properly started? These questions prompted me to write a book for complete beginners on their chakra healing journey.

This isn't simply a book that I've written to you as a reader. This is the book I've written for myself. This is the book I wish I had read when I was starting. In this book, we discussed energy healing in general, then moved on to the concepts related to chakra healing, after which we were introduced to the kundalini energy.

Then, we moved on to identifying the different effects of imbalances in our chakras. Once we were convinced of the benefits of chakra healing, we started preparing ourselves for this journey. First, we understood what we truly needed spiritually. Then, we discussed some of how we can balance our chakras. These included meditation, visualization, essential oils, sound healing, and crystals.

The last part of the book was dedicated to healing each of the first five chakras. In the end, we discussed some of the common mistakes we might make as beginners so that we can conserve our energy and make the best of this process. More than the techniques and concepts discussed, I hope that this book has given you the confidence needed to make this journey your own.

Thanks For Reading!

Hey! Thank you so much for taking the time to read this. I know you're busy, and I don't want to be too pushy, but it would mean a great deal to me if you could just take one more moment to leave me an **honest review.**

Also, don't forget to claim your **FREE** gift by scanning the code below!

References

Activating Your Chakras Using Visualisation/Meditation | al Covo, Southampton. (n.d.). Al Covo. https://www.alcovo.co.uk/blog/activating-your-chakras-using-visualisationmeditation

Anderson, S. (2018, October 1). *5 Common Misconceptions About Chakras* –. Himalayan Institute Online. https://himalayaninstitute.org/online/5-common-misconceptions-chakras/

Andrade, N. de, PhD. (2017, May 25). *How chakras affect your mental health.* Anxiety.org. https://www.anxiety.org/balance-your-chakras-let-your-anxiety-melt-away

Barkley, S. (2022, May 4). *12 Things That Prove Your Third Eye Chakra Is Blocked.* Power of Positivity: Positive Thinking & Attitude. https://www.powerofpositivity.com/third-eye-chakra-blocked/

Boswell, S. (2022, December 20). *Introduction to Chakras.* HYSSES. https://hysses.com/blogs/tips/introduction-to-chakras

Cafasso, J. (2018, September 18). *Do Binaural Beats Have Health Benefits?* Healthline. https://www.healthline.com/health/binaural-beats

Carrigan, C. (2019, September 25). *6 Common Mistakes of Energy Healers.* https://www.linkedin.com/pulse/6-common-mistakes-energy-healers-catherine-carrigan

Chakra Meditation: Unblock The 7 Chakras with Guided Meditation. (2022, December 12). https://www.anahana.com/en/meditation/chakra-meditation

Chakra Stones And Chakra Crystals - Meaning, How To Use. (2022, December 12). https://www.anahana.com/en/yoga/chakra-stones-and-chakra-crystals

Chakras & Crystals: The Ultimate Guide. (n.d.). Tiny Rituals. https://tinyrituals.co/blogs/tiny-rituals/chakra-crystals

Chakras and Yoga. (n.d.). Body & Brain. https://www.bodynbrain.com/blog/energy/chakras-and-yoga/5379

Christensen, E. (2022a, August 28). *7 Ways to Know Which Chakra Is Blocked.* wikiHow. https://www.wikihow.com/Know-Which-Chakra-Is-Blocked

Christensen, E. (2022b, December 19). *13 Easy Ways to Unblock the Solar Plexus Chakra.* wikiHow. https://www.wikihow.com/Unblock-the-Solar-Plexus-Chakra

Derfuss, M. (2021, November 29). *The 3 Most Common Mistakes Beginner Kundalini Yogis Make.* SoundWellness. https://www.soundwellness.biz/blog/2021/9/30/the-3-most-common-mistakes-beginner-kundalini-yogis-make

Discover Healing. (2019, July 1). *9 Common Misconceptions About Energy Healing.* https://discoverhealing.com/articles/9-common-misconceptions-energy-healing/

Eleanor, M. (2022, June 30). *10 Types of Energy Healing: Which One Is Right for You?* Locally Well San Diego.

https://www.locallywellsd.com/10-types-of-energy-healing-which-one-is-right-for-you/

Flavio, A. (2022, August 5). *Chakra 101: An Introduction to the 7 Chakras.* YouAlignedTM. https://youaligned.com/chakra-system-introduction/

Humphreys, K. (2022, June 6). *Chakra Visualisation.* Head & Heart Mindfulness. https://www.headandheartmindfulness.com.au/blog-items/chakravisualisation

InnerCamp. (2021, February 2). *Apply these techniques to improve chakra alignment and mental health.* InnerCamp. https://innercamp.com/apply-these-techniques-to-improve-chakra-alignment-and-mental-health/

Isaacs, N. (2021, May 4). *Is a Kundalini Awakening Safe?* Yoga Journal. https://www.yogajournal.com/yoga-101/types-of-yoga/kundalini/kundalini-awakening/

Jain, R. (2022a, November 16). *Complete Guide To The 7 Chakras: Symbols, Effects & How To Balance. Arhanta Yoga Blog.* Arhanta Yoga Ashrams. https://www.arhantayoga.org/blog/7-chakras-introduction-energy-centers-effect/

Jain, R. (2022b, December 19). *Vishuddha Chakra: How To Balance Your Throat Chakra. Arhanta Blog.* Arhanta Yoga Ashrams. https://www.arhantayoga.org/blog/vishuddha-chakra-balance-how-to-balance-your-throat-chakra/

Karana Sharira. (n.d.). Yogapedia.com. https://www.yogapedia.com/definition/7956/karana-sharira

Karya Sharira. (n.d.). Yogapedia.com. https://www.yogapedia.com/definition/7957/karya-sharira

Kerkar, P. (2018, February 28). *10 Myths About Chakras Healing*. Epainassist. https://www.epainassist.com/chakra/10-myths-about-chakras-healing

Kirby, S. (2022, October 30). *60 Chakra Quotes about Meditation and the Body*. Everyday Power. https://everydaypower.com/chakra-quotes/

Klimtchuk, K. L. (2022, August 2). *9 Ways to Open Your Spiritual Chakras*. wikiHow. https://www.wikihow.com/Open-Your-Spiritual-Chakras

Lee, A. (2020, May 25). *How To Pinpoint Exactly Which Chakra Is Out Of Balance, And How To Soothe, Activate And Balance Each*. Beyogi. https://beyogi.com/how-to-pinpoint-exactly-which-chakra-is-out-of-balance-and-how-to-soothe-activate-and-balance-each/

Lindberg, S. (2020, September 21). *9 Ways to Help Heal and Balance Your Throat Chakra*. Healthline. https://www.healthline.com/health/throat-chakra-healing

Luna, A. (2022a, October 21). *The Ultimate Guide to Solar Plexus Chakra Healing For Complete Beginners*. LonerWolf. https://lonerwolf.com/solar-plexus-chakra-healing/

Luna, A. (2022b, November 16). *What is Kundalini Awakening? (19 Intense Symptoms)*. LonerWolf. https://lonerwolf.com/kundalini-awakening/

Marshack, K. (2016, July 27). *Restore Balance by Strengthening Your Spiritual Life – Kathy J. Marshack, Ph.D.*

https://kmarshack.com/2016/07/27/restore-balance-by-strengthening-your-spiritual-life/

McGinley, K. (2021, March 22). *7 Chakra Meditations to Keep You in Balance.* Chopra. https://chopra.com/articles/7-chakra-meditations-to-keep-you-in-balance

Mercedes, M. (2022, June 13). *Unlocking the Chakras | How do you Balance the Chakras.* Power Yoga. https://poweryoga.com/the-power-in-unlocking-the-chakras/

Mindbodygreen. (2021, May 18). *15 Signs You're Having A Kundalini Awakening + What It Means.* Mindbodygreen. https://www.mindbodygreen.com/articles/kundalini-awakening

Mind is the Master. (2020, July 1). *5 Simple Ways of Knowing if your Chakras Are Blocked.* MIND IS THE MASTER. https://mindisthemaster.com/know-if-chakras-are-blocked/

Mogeni, R. (2022, September 28). *Blocked Heart Chakra: Fixing The Imbalance In Your Chakra System.* BetterMe Blog. https://betterme.world/articles/blocked-heart-chakra/

Newlyn, E. (2021, October 25). *Introduction to chakras.* Ekhart Yoga. https://www.ekhartyoga.com/articles/practice/introduction-to-chakras

Nicola Tesla Quotes. (n.d.). Goodreads. https://www.goodreads.com/author/quotes/278.Nikola_Tesla

Oils, R. M. (n.d.-a). *Exploring Your Crown Chakra.* Rocky Mountain Oils. https://www.rockymountainoils.com/learn/exploring-your-crown-chakra/

Oils, R. M. (n.d.-b). *Exploring Your Solar Plexus Chakra*. Rocky Mountain Oils. https://www.rockymountainoils.com/learn/exploring-your-solar-plexus-chakra/

Oils, R. M. (n.d.-c). *Sacral Chakra Exploring Your Second Chakra*. Rocky Mountain Oils. https://www.rockymountainoils.com/learn/exploring-your-sacral-chakra/

Patel, R. (2021, July 8). *Warning Signs Your Chakras Are Out of Balance*. Flex Studio. https://flexhk.com/blog/warning-signs-your-chakras-are-out-of-balance/

Rabbitt, M., Ezrin, S., Kirpal, V., Ezrin, S., & Lasater, J. H. (2021, September 2). *The Ultimate Guide to Energy Healing*. Yoga Journal. https://www.yogajournal.com/yoga-101/chakras-yoga-for-beginners/the-ultimate-guide-to-energy-healing/

Rishikesh, R. Y. (2021, October 16). *Complete Guide to the Chakras in Yoga*. Yoga Teacher Training in India - Raj Yoga Rishikesh. https://rajyogarishikesh.com/complete-guide-chakras.html

Ruparelia, B. . S. (n.d.). *Is Your Chakra Blocked?* Fitternity. https://www.fitternity.com/article/is-your-chakra-blocked

Schmidt, L. (2022, July 8). *5 Signs Your Chakras Are Out of Balance & How to Test Them*. Chopra. https://chopra.com/articles/5-signs-your-chakras-are-out-of-balance-and-how-to-test-them

Schweder, M. (2018, April 27). *5 Myths About The Chakras*. A Brighter Wild. https://www.abrighterwild.com/blog/5-myths-about-the-chakras

7 Chakras: Mystical Dimensions of the Body's Seven Chakras. (2021, November 15). https://isha.sadhguru.org/us/en/wisdom/article/7-chakras-mystical-dimensions-body-seven-chakras

Snyder, S. & YJ Editors. (2021a, July 30). *Everything You Need to Know About the Throat Chakra.* Yoga Journal. https://www.yogajournal.com/yoga-101/chakras-yoga-for-beginners/chakratuneup2015-intro-visuddha/

Snyder, S. & YJ Editors. (2021b, August 18). *Everything You Need to Know About the Crown Chakra.* Yoga Journal. https://www.yogajournal.com/yoga-101/chakras-yoga-for-beginners/intro-sahasrara-crown-chakra/

Solomon, P. (2021, January 10). *The balance of life.* The Daily Guardian. https://thedailyguardian.com/the-balance-of-life/

Steber, C., & Ferraro, K. (2021, June 23). *15 Signs Your Heart Chakra Is Blocked & It's Messing With Your Love Life.* Bustle. https://www.bustle.com/wellness/signs-your-heart-chakra-is-blocked-its-messing-with-your-love-life

Stelter, G. (2016, December 19). *A Beginner's Guide to the 7 Chakras and Their Meanings.* Healthline. https://www.healthline.com/health/fitness-exercise/7-chakras

Stokes, V. (2021a, February 17). *Essential Oils for Chakras: Balance and Heal with Sacred Scents.* Healthline. https://www.healthline.com/health/essential-oils-for-chakras

Stokes, V. (2021b, June 11). *Chakras and Anxiety: Find Balance to Soothe Stress, Fear, and Panic.* Healthline. https://www.healthline.com/health/mind-body/anxiety-chakra

Stokes, V. (2021c, October 25). *Root Chakra Healing: Techniques to Activate, Unblock, and Balance*. Healthline. https://www.healthline.com/health/mind-body/root-chakra-healing

Stokes, V. (2021d, December 6). *How to Balance the Sacral Chakra for Greater Sensuality, Intimacy, and Creativity*. Healthline. https://www.healthline.com/health/mind-body/sacral-chakra

Studies, T. (2022, February 17). *The real story on the Chakras*. Hareesh.org. https://hareesh.org/blog/2016/2/5/the-real-story-on-the-chakras

Sukshma Sharira. (n.d.). Yogapedia.com. https://www.yogapedia.com/definition/7968/sukshma-sharira

Sushumna. (n.d.). Yogapedia.com. https://www.yogapedia.com/definition/5596/sushumna

Team, O. (2020, October 29). *Root Chakra Healing: Everything you Need to Know - Onyx Integrative AZ*. Onyx Integrative Medicine & Aesthetics. https://onyxintegrative.com/root-chakra-healing/

Terrell, S. (2022, September 28). *How to Open Chakras for Powerful Physical and Emotional Healing*. Mindvalley Blog. https://blog.mindvalley.com/how-to-open-chakras/

The Art of Living. (2022a, March 22). *5 Common Mistakes Yoga Beginners Make*. Art of Living (India). https://www.artofliving.org/in-en/yoga/yoga-for-beginners/5-yoga-beginners-mistakes

The Art of Living. (2022b, October 14). *7 Chakras in human body, Significance & How to balance them*. Art of Living (India).

https://www.artofliving.org/in-en/meditation/meditation-benefits/seven-chakras-explained

TINT Yoga. (2019, March 21). *Pranayama: The Five Vayus.* https://tintyoga.com/magazine/pranayama-the-five-vayus/

TINT Yoga. (2020, July 13). *Chakra Yoga Explained – A Full Guide to the 7 Chakras.* https://tintyoga.com/magazine/chakra-yoga/

Top 8 Myths About Healing Crystals, Debunked. (2022, December 15). Whaler's Locker. https://whalerslocker.com/blogs/news/top-eight-myths-about-healing-crystals-debunked

YJ Editors. (2014, July 24). *Chakra-Balancing Yoga Sequence.* Yoga Journal. https://www.yogajournal.com/practice/yoga-sequences/7-poses-chakras/

YJ Editors. (2021a, March 11). *Everything You Need to Know About the Heart Chakra.* Yoga Journal. https://www.yogajournal.com/yoga-101/chakras-yoga-for-beginners/intro-heart-chakra-anahata/

YJ Editors. (2021b, April 27). *What You Need to Know About the Sacral Chakra.* Yoga Journal. https://www.yogajournal.com/yoga-101/chakras-yoga-for-beginners/intro-sacral-chakra-svadhisthana/

Yogashop. (n.d.). *BLOG - The Yoga Chakras: What are chakras and how does this work?* https://www.yogashop.nl/en/blogs/yoga-en-meditatie/the-yoga-chakras-what-are-chakras-and-how-does-thi/

Yugay, I. (2022, September 28). *How to Identify the Symptoms of Blocked Chakras.* Mindvalley Blog. https://blog.mindvalley.com/symptoms-of-blocked-chakras/

Made in the USA
Middletown, DE
03 June 2023

32001903R00075